A Gang
of
Pecksniffs

Books by Theo Lippman, Jr.

A Gang of Pecksniffs (Editor)
Spiro Agnew's America
Muskie (With Donald C. Hansen)

A Gang
of
Pecksniffs

AND OTHER COMMENTS ON NEWSPAPER PUBLISHERS, EDITORS AND REPORTERS

BY H.L. MENCKEN

**SELECTED, EDITED AND INTRODUCED
WITH A PROFILE OF MENCKEN AS NEWSMAN
BY THEO LIPPMAN, JR.**

ARLINGTON HOUSE·PUBLISHERS
NEW ROCHELLE, NEW YORK

Manufactured in the United States of America

Library of Congress Cataloging in Publication Data

Mencken, Henry Louis, 1880-1956.
   A gang of pecksniffs.

    1. Journalism--Collected works. I. Title.
PN4733.M45   070.4'092'4   75-17980
ISBN 0-87000-320-8

This book is for Madeline

Contents

A Gang of Pecksniffs

Acknowledgments

My first and greatest debt is to my wife Madeline, whose idea this book was and who did much of the research and typing for it. I would like to name all of my colleagues at the *Sunpapers* who shared with me their memories of working with Mencken, but there were so very many, my list will surely inadvertently be incomplete. I must give special thanks to the following present or former *Sunpapers* men who provided me with personal papers or other such research material: William M. Bernard, Gary Black, Jr., R. P. Harriss, Gerald Johnson, Donald Kirkley, Frederic Nelson, Gwinn Owens, Maclean Patterson, Fred Rasmussen, and Clem Vitek. An H. L. Mencken Room is maintained by the Humanities Department of the Enoch Pratt Free Library. I owe more than I can express to the staff of that department, particularly Richard Hart and the late Betty Adler. Mr. William G. Frederick of the Mercantile-Safe Deposit and Trust Co., which is trustee under Mr. Mencken's will, was gracious in his dealings with me, and I am indebted to the estate for permission to reprint here a great deal of previously unpublished material. "Journalism in America," copyright 1927 by Alfred A. Knopf, Inc., and renewed 1955 by H. L. Mencken, is reprinted from *Prejudices: A Selection,* by H. L. Mencken, edited by James T. Farrell, by permission of the publisher. For my introduction, "The Life of Kings," I drew on interviews; letters to and from Mencken at the Pratt, the New York Public Library, and the University of Virginia Library; fragments of memoirs and other writing by Mencken at the Pratt and the New York Public Library; the Pratt's magazine *Menckeniana*; a pamphlet, "H. L. Mencken," written by Philip Wagner for the University of Minnesota in 1966; three biographies, *Mencken,* by Carl Bode (Southern Illinois University Press, 1968), *The Irreverent Mr. Mencken,* by Edgar Kemler (Little, Brown and Company, 1950), and *Disturber of the Peace,* by William Manchester (Harper and Brothers, 1950); and three autobiographical works, *Happy Days, Newspaper Days, Heathen Days* (Knopf, 1940, 1941, 1943).

THEO LIPPMAN, JR.
BALTIMORE, JANUARY 1975

Introduction:

"The Life of Kings"

by
Theo Lippman, Jr.

I

In June 1943 H. L. Mencken sent a confidential handwritten note to his old friend Edgar Ellis, the librarian of the Baltimore *Sunpapers.* It asked Ellis to place in Mencken's morgue envelope instructions to some future obituary writer. He told Ellis he could read the note but "*Keep it to yourself.*" The typed-out instructions said, "Save in the event that the circumstances of my death make necessary a news story, it is my earnest request to my old colleagues of the *Sunpapers* that they print only a very brief announcement of it, with no attempt at a biographical sketch, no portrait, and no editorial." The note was signed with his familiar scrawl. Mencken supplied a small envelope with the legend, "To whoever covers my death." Ellis put the note in the envelope, sealed it with five dabs of black wax, and placed it in Mencken's file in the morgue. True to his friend's instructions, he told no one what the envelope contained. This spurred quite a guessing game around the *Sunpapers* once the existence of the envelope became known. The two favorite guesses were that the envelope contained (1) "the goods on Jack Pollack," a Baltimore politician with a shady history, and (2) a blank sheet of paper. Mencken knew more

13

about Baltimore exotics than he ever wrote, and he loved a gag, so either was a good possibility. The tantalizing sealed envelope was soon taken out of the library, whence almost anyone could have removed it, and locked in a small metal box on Ellis's desk. The managing editors of *The Sun* and *The Evening Sun* were given keys and told to read the letter immediately on Mencken's death.

On a Sunday morning, January 30, 1956, Mencken died, the envelope was opened, and, of course, snorted at as Mencken must have known it would be. Obituaries had long since been prepared. If Mencken had been merely a newspaperman, his death would still have been worthy of extended comment in Baltimore and elsewhere. He was one of the most influential and best-known journalists of his day. He had been a giant on the *Sunpapers* for more than 40 years, and he had edited another Baltimore paper before joining *The Sun*. But, of course, he was more than a newspaperman. "Editor," "Critic," "Author" appeared in the headlines announcing his death in papers around the world; more often, in fact, than did "Newspaperman" or "Journalist." *The Sun*'s headline said "H. L. Mencken, Author, Dies at 75," though the first paragraph of the story identified him as "newspaper man, critic, wit and Baltimore's best-known writer." Mencken would have understood the headline writer's problem. Words have to fit a certain space. He wrote his own headlines for years before giving it up late in the '30s. "The copy desk does it better," he told a friend.

The Sun for Monday, January 31, 1956, ignored Mencken's posthumous request on all counts. There was a column-long news story; a five-column obituary written by Hamilton Owens, the editor in chief; an editorial; and a full page of pictures. The news story, the obit, and one picture were on Page One, which was unusual for *The Sun*. Only truly shattering local events were put on Page One in those days. Mencken's death was still overshadowed by local stories on the front page that day. Two other local stories were also out front, an unprecedented occurrence. One was the city's first bus strike, the other was a fire at an auditorium in which ten people were burned to death. Every member of the local staff was called into the city room to cover the news. It was a hectic, Hollywoodish day; a fitting sendoff to Mencken, who would have loved it. One of his favorite yarns had to do with his directing the coverage of the great Baltimore fire in 1904.

14

It wasn't just fires, though—he loved all newspaper work, particularly covering stories. Only a few years before he died he read an article by Stanley Walker on "What Makes a Good Reporter." Walker mentioned Mencken as one of the best. "Dear Stanley," Mencken wrote him, ". . . as I look back over a misspent life, I find myself more and more convinced that I had more fun doing news reporting than in any other enterprise. It is really the life of kings."

II

Harry Mencken, son of a prosperous Baltimore tobacco merchant, became H. L. Mencken, future newspaperman, at the age of nine. His father had bought him a printing press that Christmas, and he then accidentally ruined the "r's." So the young Mencken began printing his name H. L. Mencken. Before he finished high school eight years later he had decided he wanted only to join the staff of the *Morning Herald.* No other career appealed to him. He prepared for this life by reading everything he could get his hands on in the Enoch Pratt Free Library, finding the most nourishment in *Steps into Journalism*, by Edwin J. Shuman, an editorial writer for the Chicago *Tribune.* He also took a correspondence course. He had a high school friend who could get him entree to the *Herald.* But father said "no." He could join the family firm or go to college and prepare for a professional career—but no newspaper job. Young Mencken took the tobacco business and stayed at it until his father died in 1899. Within days he had applied for a job on the *Herald*, and within weeks was hard at work there. He rose rapidly to police reporter while still 18, to City Hall reporter at 19, to star, assigned to all the big stories, by the time he was 20. At 21 he was Sunday editor; at 23, city editor; and at 25, editor.

The *Herald* was in poor condition by then. The able city editor who had hired Mencken, Max Ways, had left, and the reportorial staff was composed of men mostly a generation ahead of Mencken and yet far below him in ability. The young city editor took charge, firing about ten reporters, hiring new ones, constantly rewriting the stories of those who couldn't write the way he wanted them to. His model was again an editorial writer, Edward M. Kingsbury, on the staff of the New York *Sun.* Years later Mencken tried to get an article about Kingsbury in the *American Mercury.* Kingsbury, by then a Pulitzer Prize winner, was an extremely shy man and begged off. Out of respect for his privacy, Mencken dropped the project.

Mencken thought he was a better city editor than he was a reporter. Once, for a friend, he assessed his work in those years and concluded that he was not a good reporter at all. But he was, even in the textbook sense of getting to the scene early, getting everybody's middle initial, spelling names right. The *Herald*, in those days, was no match for the Baltimore *Sun*, which was an older, more prosperous paper with a larger staff. It was also very sobersided. As a reporter, and later as city editor, Mencken felt compelled to accentuate breezy writing and scoops in an effort to compete for readers with the *Sun.* He enjoyed and stuck to the former (he called *Sun* reporters "bookkeepers"), but he disdained scoops. Most scoops were bad stories in his opinion, then and later. Though Mencken occasionally depreciated his reporting skills, he could also take offense at suggestions that he was not really a reporter. In 1936, when he was asked by the Associated Press to write an article on how it felt "to be out on the firing line again," Mencken replied that he had never left the firing line in the first place and that reporting had not changed much. "The telephone had affected [reporters'] work, of course, but not to the extent that newspapermen seem to think." Good reporters, he told a friend, did better under primitive conditions anyway.

The *Herald* had a clean, modern, efficient building with two telephones (one furnished by each of the competing telephone companies in Baltimore). The phones were seldom used, however. Deadlines were no problem on the *Herald*, since the first edition was seldom printed until after midnight. Extras were unheard of— until the great fire of 1904. Late one February Sunday morning, Mencken was snoring away at home, after a long night at work and in an after-hours saloon, when he received a phone call from one of the older reporters on the *Herald* alerting him that a big fire had broken out downtown. A little later another reporter came to fetch him, with the good news that it looked like a "humdinger." It was, a 21-alarm fire that destroyed most of downtown, including the *Herald* building. Mencken directed news coverage, wrote headlines, edited copy; beginning in Baltimore, then in offices of the

Washington *Post* when the *Herald* building had to be abandoned, then in the offices of the Philadelphia *Evening Telegraph*. It was five weeks before the *Herald* staff returned to Baltimore to work, in a car barn. Mencken worked nearly 72 hours straight at the worst of the fire. "I came out of it . . . a middle-aged man," he later recalled in his autobiography. "Middle-aged" was too dramatic. A surer description was Mencken's earlier, private one, that the fire made him "a grown man." He was, after all, just 23.

The *Herald* came out of it much aged, too, and not for the better. Within two and a half years, the *Herald* ceased to exist. Mencken had become editor by then. He leapt from the wreckage to the Baltimore *Evening News* for a brief stint as news editor, then to the *Sun* as Sunday editor. That same year, 1906, Carr van Adna of the New York *Times*, an old *Sun* man, wrote Mencken offering him a job there. Mencken refused, and he and the *Sun* began an intimate relationship that lasted the rest of his life.

III

The *Sun* was a staid, rich, and powerful newspaper in Baltimore when Mencken joined it, already nearly 70 years old. It then published mornings and Sundays, and soon would add an evening edition. It was a conservative paper, journalistically, having only hired its first columnist two months before Mencken joined the staff, its first advertising salesman a year before. As Sunday editor, Mencken was paid $40 a week, oversaw a staff of two, and had a budget of $100 for free-lance writers and artists. Mencken wrote some editorials, and here appeared the first portents of the national gadfly Mencken would become, to the puzzlement of some regular readers of the *Sun*. Here also appeared the first portents of the adviser to publishers and editors Mencken was to become in later years. The *Sun* then was still so old-fashioned as not to reveal its circulation figures. Mencken pointed out to his superiors that this prevented him, as an editor, from keeping up with "how I was doing." Eventually the paper's managers decided to begin making the information known to some advertisers and editors.

Much of the change that was to take place at the *Sun* came after 1910, when Charles H. Grasty, the man who had owned the *News*, bought control of the *Sun*. Mencken thought he might be fired, since he had walked out on Grasty to come to the *Sun* in the first place. But Grasty asked him to stay to help ease the transition. Grasty knew he was suspect in the eyes of many of the veterans of the *Sun* staff, and so needed an ambassador. But he wanted more than an ambassador in Mencken. He respected the not-yet-30-year-old's executive journalistic abilities. He told Mencken he wanted him to calm the fears of the old hands, and to enlarge the Sunday paper *and* start an afternoon edition of the *Sun*. The *Evening Sun,* which never attained the national reputation that its older morning sister did, became Mencken's real home base for most of the rest of his career. It began publication in the spring of 1910, with Mencken serving as principal assistant to the new editor, John Haslup Adams. Mencken did at least half of the writing for the editorial page each day—anonymous editorials and initialed pieces on a whole range of subjects. The latter caught the eye of one of the owners of the papers, a youthful Harry C. Black. Black had been studying in England, where he became a fan of the irreverent columns of Harry Bottemley. Black suggested to Grasty that H. L. M., whom he did not know, ought to be given the opportunity of writing a similar column. He believed a little irreverence and personality were just what the new paper needed.

Bylined columns were relatively rare in American journalism at that time. The *Sun,* as noted, had only hired its first in 1906. There were no real syndicated columnists. Bylines of any sort were rare for staff writers in those days. Famous writers were occasionally hired to cover important national events for a group of newspapers. The byline usually came after the public reputation was made. For Mencken and the handful of other daily columnists of the pre-World War I period the reverse was true. However, in an age when there was no radio, television, or widely read magazines, a local reputation could be quickly won by a talented writer. Particularly one as outrageous as Mencken proved to be in the Free Lance.

The Free Lance began in May 1911. Mencken had written a column of sorts for a while at the *News,* but it was nothing like what the Free Lance was to become. The new column was marked by its tone of witty criticism of almost every institution newspaper readers were accustomed to seeing treated with grave respect, particularly in the *Sun.* Mencken blasted politicians, civil servants, businessmen, preachers, professional men . . . everybody. His column was full of exotic words—many foreign ones that few readers could be expected to understand. Yet the columns were never vague or confusing for all of that. In fact it was always Mencken's boast about the column (and later newspaper writing) that it was very easy to read. Nor was the column predictable. Some days it would be a combination of, say, statistics proving Baltimore was failing in some endeavor, an essay on music or food, some sly dig at critics of Germany (as war approached), perhaps a brief comment on new words, a joke or two. Other days the entire column might be devoted to a straight description of some cityscape. Other days he would write of a new love, the language of Americans. Even when there were no arch comments or devilish criticisms, the Mencken style, unique and so recognizable, was a reminder that anything was possible, and the next paragraph might include any sort of surprise. A glance through the four years of the Free Lance shows column after column campaigning for hygienic reforms in typhoid-conscious Baltimore. It was a serious campaign, though some readers must have wondered. His target was a foot-dragging city government. He attacked with sarcasm, indirectly. "Boil your drinking water!" was a repeated warning, followed by such nonsense as "Revere the City Council!" or "Don't Rock the boat!" There was always a playfulness in the column. Once he ended it in mid-sentence, to be resumed the next day. Once he devoted the column to simple reprinting of city conflict-of-interest ordinances—with the type arranged so as to leave squares of blank spaces. "Loopholes," he pointed out.

The column occasionally was padded with public relations handouts, but never to the point that anyone could have accused Mencken of neglecting his job of gathering and writing. Years later Mencken complained in his private journal that Franklin P. Adams, who was writing a similar column in the New York *Tribune* at the time, failed as a columnist because he was lazy and filled his column with contributions. "Stirring up the animals," as Mencken called his columning, became a chore after four years. He was also doing other things, including special assignments for the morning, evening, and Sunday *Sunpapers,* and work on books. He was also coeditor of the *Smart Set* magazine. Mencken found the column a burden. For a dynamo like Mencken, the work load itself was probably tolerable. What wasn't was that his decidedly pro-German views were leading him down a very different path from that Adams and the other *Sun* editors were taking. The *Sunpapers* were strong supporters of Woodrow Wilson and the Allied cause in the war. Mencken detested Wilson and hated the British, or at least the British war aims, and often said so, pugnaciously, in the Free Lance. Mencken also delighted in "stirring up the animals" by throwing more and more German words into the Free Lance's paragraphs. He tired of it all by October 1915, gave up the column and half his $50-a-week salary.

IV

The cut in salary was no hardship at the time. Mencken's income from his other writings was more than enough for his needs. His father's estate provided comfortably for his mother and sister. After a year of writing only occasional articles for the *Sunpapers,* he arranged to go to Germany to report the progress of the war, both for the *Sunday Sun* and the North American Newspaper Alliance. He sailed for Germany as 1916 ended and America's entry in the war on the side of the Allies seemed certain. Even in heavily German Baltimore the act of sending Mencken to report on Germany seemed unpatriotic to many readers. The *Sun* ran ads and editorial explanations, stressing, not playing down, Mencken's pro-German bias. The Sunday paper carried a first dispatch on January 28, 1917. Mencken's article was datelined Berlin and described Germans as united in their fight for "freedom and their right to exist as a nation." The paper described the Mencken article pointedly as "a letter," and balanced it with a pro-Allies dispatch from London from another nonstaff member, Norman Hapgood. Mencken stayed in Germany until the United States broke off diplomatic relations in March. Then he sailed to Cuba to report on the revolution there. The Mencken articles were front page items in the *Sunpapers* and, through NANA, in papers in New York, Chicago, Philadelphia, St. Louis, Boston, and other large cities. He saw some combat ("as little as a state commander of the American Legion") but was more impressed by the bitter cold than any other dangers. Many of the articles appeared after Mencken had fled Europe. He kept a diary and filed excerpts from it.

With America entering the war shortly after Mencken returned, his continued writing for the *Sun,* even as an outsider, was impossible. So was his writing for almost any paper. One exception, perhaps the only one, was the New York *Evening Mail.* Its publisher was the pro-German Dr. Edward A. Rumely. Mencken was asked to contribute two articles a week on any subject not related to war, patriotism, etc. John Cullen, the managing editor of the *Evening Mail,* had known Mencken in Baltimore. He implored Mencken to keep the articles humorous and light. The pay was supposed to be $15 per article, but often the editors at the paper would split one manuscript into two articles. Bookkeeping was erratic and Mencken never received the pay to which he was entitled. Though his articles avoided dangerous topics, both he and the paper were still suspect in the eyes of the law. Mencken was interviewed by government agents about his views and friends. Rumely eventually lost the paper and went to jail.

Surprisingly, the *Evening Mail* articles were of more than lasting interest, dealing with literature, manners, medicine, education, and so forth. Two of them turned out to be among the most famous articles Mencken ever wrote for newspapers: "The Sahara of the Bozart," an attack on the South that was to lead to a lifelong feud between the urban Marylander and the rural-oriented South, and "A Neglected Anniversary," a hoax concerning the history of the bath tub in America. The quality of the articles was not a source of pride or comfort to the writer at the time, however, because he was forbidden to do what he liked to do best in newspapers, comment on the news of the hour. When he occasionally tried to slip in a column dealing even peripherally with the war, as for instance one on censorship, it was killed. It was therefore a special relief for Mencken to see the war end and to be invited back to the *Sunpapers* in 1919.

V

One of Mencken's deskmates and friends in the early days at the *Evening Sun* was Paul Patterson, managing editor of the young

21

paper. He soon switched to the business and financial side of the paper's management. In September 1919 he was told he would shortly be named president of the company publishing the *Sunpapers,* with a mandate to make them into papers of national renown and influence. Patterson called on Mencken for advice. They began meeting several nights a week with Harry C. Black to plan the future editorial thrust and operations of the three *Suns.* Mencken had his *Smart Set* editing chores and other writing assignments, but he was still living and working in Baltimore. He came back to the *Sunpapers* as an editorial consultant and columnist at $5,000 a year. Even if he had been *only* a consultant, the *Sunpapers* would have made a good bargain. There was hardly an important management decision without benefit of Mencken's thinking. (It wasn't always followed, of course.) Patterson made it a habit to ask Mencken "Would you think this over?" when some change was in the air. Mencken advised Patterson on policies and personnel. He had a wide range of friendships in the newspaper world, particularly after he became editor of the *American Mercury* in 1924 and began cultivating newspapermen as contributors. It was through Mencken that the political cartoonist Edmund Duffy came to the *Sun.* Gerald Johnson came to the *Evening Sun* from North Carolina after catching Mencken's eye by criticizing his anti-Southern articles.

Mencken had no title or office at the *Sunpapers,* but he came to the building almost every afternoon for the editorial conferences in Patterson's office. John Owens, who became editor of the *Sun* in 1927, later recalled that "I thought of him as editor of the *Sun.*" Hamilton Owens, who became editor of the *Evening Sun* in 1922 when he was only 34 years old, later gave Mencken the highest praise for his counsel: "From the very first he recognized that, with all the good intentions in the world, I was too inexperienced to be capable of doing a good job. So he set out to help and support me. He would come into my office nearly every afternoon and sit around for a half hour or so, delighting me with his explosive conversation and perhaps, more than I realized at the time, guiding my own thinking into channels more or less like his own. The editorial page of the Baltimore *Evening Sun* in those far off days gained a reputation for being at worst smart-alecky and at best witty and pungent. Most of it was due to Mencken." Interestingly,

Mencken's political philosophy was often at odds with that of both editorial pages in the '20s and '30s. Until the *Sun* turned against Roosevelt during the New Deal, the editorial pages were more or less liberal. When Mencken's conversation on political issues failed to influence either of the Owenses or their successors, he would not press it. Hamilton Owens liked to quote Mencken as saying, "You're the jail editor," meaning that Owens, not Mencken, was responsible in every way for what went on the page.

One famous argument that Mencken lost was over whether the staid old *Sun's* editorial page should be jazzed up. In the summer of 1928 Paul Patterson asked Mencken to read the editorial page closely with an eye to suggesting changes. Mencken finished the chore while in New York and wrote Patterson a six-and-a-half-page letter discussing almost every detail of the page, from typography to cartooning to letters to the editor. His strongest language he reserved for the content of the editorials themselves. "Too cautious . . . excess of politeness . . . It is also useful to remember that most men are convinced, not by appeals to their reason, but by appeals to their emotions and prejudices. Such emotions and prejudices are not necessarily ignoble. It is just as creditable to hate injustice and dishonesty as it is to love the truth. One of the chief purposes of the *Sun*, as I understand it, is to stir up such useful hatreds." Owens replied, ". . . This paper has set itself up as liberal. . . . If liberalism means anything, it means that kind of intellectual honesty which opens the doors to all the facts." Mencken did not pursue it.

Mencken was an idea man for the news as well as the editorial operations. He was forever suggesting that a certain story be investigated, either by a staff man or by some newspaperman in a far-off city. He read many papers. Every time he came across a good story, he would note the by-line and drop a note to one of the editors at the *Sunpapers*, saying, "If you ever need a good man in such and such a city, so and so does a fine job."

The management of the *Sunpapers* also called on Mencken during this period between the wars for noneditorial assistance. It was Mencken who pressed the *Evening Sun*'s case when it was trying to get an Associated Press franchise in the '20s. And, ironically, considering his own reputation for angering churchmen, it was to Mencken the company turned when a Catholic boycott of the *Sunpapers* cut sharply into circulation in the '30s. The boycott was the result of the *Sun*'s Berlin correspondent's comparing Hitler to Saint Ignatius Loyola. Mencken went to the apostolic delegate to Washington and got him to appeal to the Baltimore archbishop who was leading the crusade against the *Sun*. Mencken also eased the way for the *Sun* to issue an apology of sorts to the Catholics.

A few months later, in October 1934, Mencken was named to the Board of Directors of the A. S. Abell Co., which published the *Sunpapers*. It was a strange appointment in a sense. Editorial and news matters were almost never discussed at board meetings (though board members discussed such matters informally and with gusto at the luncheons that preceded the meetings), Mencken had very little stock in the company, and he certainly had little expertise in corporate financial matters. Nevertheless he remained a board member until his retirement after World War II. He was conservative in all senses, opposing the construction of a new building and the acquiring of a television franchise. Probably his most important chore, from the point of view of some board members, was his representation of the company in the negotiations with the newly founded American Newspaper Guild. Mencken argued strongly in favor of excluding editorial workers from the Guild jurisdiction. He loathed the New York columnist Heywood Broun ("an old quack" he called him once) who was the guiding spirit of the Guild then, but he did not seriously object to the local representatives. He told several out-of-town editors and publishers during the period that he found the negotiations pleasant and interesting. Eventually the Guild won its fight with the *Sunpapers*, but that was after Mencken was no longer acting in management's behalf.

To a lesser degree Mencken served through the two decades as an adviser or friend to managements at other newspapers. This was particularly true in regard to employment. Uncounted times he helped get a man and a job together. Perhaps his most famous success in this was sending James M. Cain to Walter Lippmann at the new York *World*. Herbert Bayard Swope, who ran the *World*, used Mencken's articles when he could, and also his ideas about coverage. They were forever exchanging ideas about general and specific problems. When the new Chicago *Sun* was launched in

1941, the editor invited Mencken to attend the ceremonies, then later asked him to read the paper and "let me know what you think of it." Grover Hall, the Alabama editor, often appealed to Mencken for advice. When his paper was sold, Hall sought Mencken's help in finding another job. Mrs. Julian Harris often sought Mencken's help in connection with her and her husband's and her son's newspaper work in the South. Mencken and Doris Fleeson were close friends from the '30s till his death. He advised her on job opportunities and stories, as well as on family matters. Throughout the rough depression years reporters and editors less fortunate than Miss Fleeson were calling on Mencken to get them jobs at the *Sunpapers* or elsewhere. His record on this score does not seem to have been too good, but his correspondence files show that he almost always made the effort. The *Sun* was not hiring; he had to write time and again, "I suggest you write so and so" or "I hear they are looking for a desk man in such and such . . ." He even peddled books for fellow journalists. He steered several reporters with manuscripts to book publishers he knew, often first reading the work himself.

Even if Mencken had never written a word for newspapers in the period after he came back to the *Sunpapers,* he would have been a significant figure in American journalism. But, of course, he did write.

VI

On February 9, 1920, a Monday, there appeared the first of some 800 "Monday Articles" that Mencken wrote for the *Evening Sun* editorial page over the next 18 years. He seldom missed a Monday, writing from hospitals, trains, ships, homes of friends, political conventions, everywhere—except in the *Sun* building itself. Mencken was most comfortable writing at home, the Hollins Street row house in which he lived practically all of his life. He was in the *Sun* offices every day he was in Baltimore, so he would serve as his own messenger and bring in the copy, usually early in the week before it was due to appear. When he was out of town he would mail in the column well in advance of deadline. Often he would mail in late corrections as well, trusting the U. S. Post Office to save him from a bad choice of a word or words. He kept his carbons, not only until the columns were safely in type, but for his archives. Practically all the Monday Articles are today pasted up in scrapbooks in the Enoch Pratt Free Library in Baltimore—carbons of the typescripts that can be compared with the clippings from the paper, also in the scrapbooks. As a general rule Mencken wrote very clean copy. The placement in the paper was always the same: a squared-off two columns in the center of the page at the top, under a short headline in half-inch-high type, then the byline, then a copyright line.

Mencken was a careful writer who needed very little editing. "Meticulous on facts and spelling—that was the old city editor in him," says Gerald Johnson, who edited the columns for a few years. (And who, at Mencken's suggestion, wrote "Thursday Articles" that were as liberal regarding politics as Mencken's were conservative.) Mencken himself was a sharp editor of other writers' copy. Philip Wagner, who later became editor of the *Evening Sun* and then the *Sun,* once wrote an article for Mencken's *American Mercury,* the entire lead of which Mencken rewrote. Later we shall see how Mencken edited other writers when he was briefly editor of the *Evening Sun.* Mencken did not object to being edited. He once told Hearst editors, when he was writing a column for that chain, to edit as they saw fit. On the *Evening Sun* editors knew they were free to edit—but they also knew Mencken would have the last word if the editing was wrong. Hamilton Owens liked to tell the story about the time he excised from a Monday Article the prediction that ministers were so against alcoholic beverages (this during prohibition) that they would substitute Coca-Cola for grape juice in communion. "Too far-fetched," Owens told Mencken after the fact. Mencken didn't say anything then, but later sent Owens a testimonial advertisement from a Western paper in which a preacher said he *had* switched to the soft drink for the sacrament. Mencken's famous Monday obituary of William Jennings Bryan was apparently edited somewhat severely between editions. The carbon of the copy is not available. The published version that is in the *Evening Sun* (and Enoch Pratt) files does not justify some of the specific criticism of it that appeared in letters to the editor later that week. Francis Bierne, the editorial writer who edited that column, recalled, years later, that it was so shocking in its attack on Bryan that he and the other editors believed Mencken was unaware that Bryan had died. Finally they went ahead with the column, but had second thoughts when they saw it in type. Then, he said, they watered it down.

Editing of Mencken for purposes of policy or business was rare. A few of the Monday Articles submitted by Mencken over the years were turned down, but these decisions were made by the editors, not higher ups, as far as anyone could tell. In 1938 Mencken wrote Charles Ross of the St. Louis *Post-Dispatch,* "I don't recall a single instance of the business office attempting any interference with an editorial matter. This sounds somewhat smug, but it is a plain fact."

Almost no topic was out of bounds in the Monday Articles; almost no target too big or small. Mencken wrote about (usually critically) the South, prohibition, the churches, education, businessmen, banks, the government, the Klan, international affairs, the stock market, journalism, police, war, beer, food, farmers, and, of course, politics, but seldom about one of his favorite topics, literature. The copyright line, with its stern warning about reprinting without permission, was necessary because Mencken was at the height of his fame during this period and his attacks were newsworthy. When he lambasted Arkansas, the state's legislature tried to get him deported. His criticisms of other Southern states were not quite so effective in stirring up criticisms, but almost. Mencken had early understood the value of being a target. When he was writing the Free Lance column, he was also editing letters to the editor. He gave priority to attacks on his writing. He liked to see such attacks in the '20s and '30s, too. Once, in the mid-'20s, when an anonymous letter writer ridiculed his pro-German views, Mencken cried out to the editors that he would have revenge. He was genuinely angry, but that was the exception to the rule.

Perhaps the most heated reaction to the Mencken columns came not from some far-off state legislature or church council or prohibitionist organization, but from the people of Mencken's own state. A great many of his Monday Articles dealt with local matters: reminiscences of Baltimore, city and state politicians, Maryland cuisine, the Johns Hopkins University. He also liked to chide the Eastern Shore of Maryland, which was then isolated, rural, poor, and Southern. In December 1931 he wrote three columns excoriating the people of the Eastern Shore for the lynching of a Negro. This led to a Shore businessmen's boycott of the *Sunpapers'* advertising columns, many cancellations of subscriptions, scores of vitriolic letters to the editor that included threats of physical violence, actual attacks on *Sunpapers* trucks on the Shore. A friend of Mencken's who lived on the Shore warned him, in all seriousness, that he might be killed if he ventured there in the next 20 years.

VII

Mencken had a pretty inflexible work schedule during these years. At work in his study by nine, for two hours with his secretary on his mail. Lunch. *Sunpapers* building for meetings with the editors. Back home by 3:30, there to work till five on writing and filing. Five to six he would read books (always lying down on a favorite sofa). A walk to mail his letters. Supper. Writing from 7:45 till ten. An hour with his brother August, drinking beer and talking. Read in bed from eleven till late. Not all of the writing that Mencken was doing every afternoon and evening in his study on Hollins Street was for the Monday Articles. He was editing his magazines, writing book reviews and other articles for his and other magazines, working on his books, and also writing for other sections of the *Sunpapers* or for other newspapers. Only a month after the first Monday Article appeared, there was a Mencken byline over a page-one report on President Harding's inauguration. That summer of 1921 Mencken covered the Dempsey-Carpentier fight for the *Evening Sun* and the New York *World,* filing four stories. Also in 1921, for page one of the *Evening Sun,* he wrote an assessment of the Sacco-Vanzetti case. Throughout the Monday Articles period, the *Sun* and *Evening Sun* would carry such Mencken pieces as obituaries (usually of journalists), anonymous editorials, book reviews, reporting on international conferences such as the London Naval Conference of 1930, and, in 1925, a series of reports on the famous Monkey Trial. That trial, involving a Dayton, Tennessee, high school teacher who taught about the theory of evolution (though it was against Tennessee law), was the first great media event. Each *Sunpaper* sent two reporters, top men —Frank Kent and Fred Essary for the *Sun,* Mencken and Henry Hyde for the *Evening Sun.* Mencken also helped talk Clarence Darrow into defending the school teacher. The prosecution was assisted by William Jennings Bryan. The papers put up the teacher's bond; when the state won its case the papers paid his fine. Mencken filed several dispatches that the *Evening Sun* ran as front-page commentaries, to go along with Hyde's sober reporting. Mencken displayed all his dislike for religion, prohibition, rural and Southern mores, Bryan, and narrow-mindedness and censorship. These articles, even more than earlier columns attacking the South such as "The Sahara of the Bozart," angered Southerners, including the conservative intellectuals who might otherwise have found much in Mencken to agree with.

Meanwhile Mencken had begun to write a Sunday column for the Chicago *Tribune* and its syndicate. These articles also appeared in the *Evening Sun* on the Saturday before they appeared elsewhere. So from late 1924, when the column began, until early 1928, when he had to give it up as too onerous, Mencken was appearing in the *Evening Sun* at least twice a week, and once a week in the influential *Tribune* and some 30 other papers in the United States and a couple of foreign countries. The articles originally were supposed to emphasize literary matters, but Mencken soon was writing about politics, religion, and other subjects guaranteed to "stir up the animals." A great many of these articles later found their way, in rewritten form, into the Prejudices series of books. While it lasted, the syndication was a rewarding one for Mencken. It meant he was reaching an audience in the major cities. Once he attempted to withdraw the column from the Boston *Herald* because the editor—"a rotten coward," bellowed Mencken— attacked Mencken during a censorship trial there involving the *American Mercury.* When the paper would not give up its rights to Mencken, he instructed the *Tribune* syndicate first to keep that portion of his income, and then to divert it to the American Civil Liberties Union. His income from the syndicate was something like $500 a week at its peak. This was at a time when Mencken's salary at the *Sunpapers* was still only $5,000 a year.

Mencken began writing for Hearst in 1934. This was a series of weekly articles dealing with the American language. They appeared for a year on the popular opposite-editorial-page of the Heart flagship paper, the New York *American,* and in all the rest of the Hearst chain except the Baltimore link. Mencken told friends he wouldn't write for a Hearst editorial page itself. But he did not tell that to Hearst or his top aides. Just before he began the *American* series, he was approached by Arthur Brisbane, Hearst's prize political columnist, and asked to write a daily column "of frank comments on events of the day." Mencken said he could not do it at the time, but maybe later. Two years later, in the summer of 1936, another Hearst official called on Mencken, told him Brisbane was ill, and that Hearst wanted Mencken to take over the column at $1,000 a week. Mencken thought it over, then told Hearst that, while he was "sorely tempted," he had decided to stay with the *Sunpapers,* "an integral part of my life for 30 years."

VIII

Mencken's first Monday Article, headlined "A Carnival of Buncombe," was devoted to his favorite journalistic subject, presidential politics. About 10 percent of the Monday Articles over the years dealt with presidential politics or performance, and Mencken's writings about these topics were not limited to the Monday Articles. He began covering the national political scene before he joined the *Sun,* in a period when few papers sent their own men to presidential nominating conventions, and he was still covering presidential conventions and campaigns in 1948 when he was three years past the normal retirement age. Some of his greatest defeats and victories, and many of his closest friendships resulted from his years at conventions, on campaign trains, in packed auditoriums. For almost all the first half of the century, Mencken was a part of that environment. He made even more newspaper friends through this activity than he did as editor of the *American Mercury.* He was not strictly a reporter anymore, nor even, for that matter, a "straight" political columnist. The latter calling was a new one in America in the years following World War I. The pioneers were Walter Lippmann at the New York *Herald-Tribune,* Mencken's colleague at the *Sun,* Frank Kent, and just a handful of others. Occasionally Mencken's editorial page articles were similar to Lippmann's and Kent's work in approach, but his front page dispatches were unique. His being there was as much a part of the story as the story he was covering itself. It was a case of the messenger being as important as the message. Some headlines through the year demonstrate that:

> McAdoo a Corpse, But,
> To Mencken's Surprise,
> Won't Go in the Grave

> Air of Deceit and Fraud
> Pervades Whole G.O.P.
> Meeting, Says Mencken

> Tragedy of Meeting,
> To Mencken, Is the
> Collapse of Al Smith

These were very long stories running to 2,000 and 3,000 words. They were full of Mencken opinions, but they were also fact-filled and highly descriptive in those pretelevision days, the result of great effort and time. His peers knew him as a hard worker. He was a familiar figure on campaign trains and in convention halls, rushing to every meeting or speech, or banging away at his typewriter right up to deadline. He was an extremely fast two-, three-, and four-fingered typist. He rewrote for every edition—new leads, adds, changes, corrections. When his deadlines were past for the day, he would do the legwork for his *Sunpapers'* colleagues writing for the next cycle. His peers also knew the results of his hard work were good journalism. This was true on into the '30s and '40s when most reporters had become far more liberal politically than Mencken could even conceive of. It was ironic that what the general public looked for in Mencken's reports from the political wars was Mencken himself, but what his fellow journalists looked for was the reportage itself. Copies of the *Sun* and *Evening Sun* were hot items in the convention city hotels. Every four years, just before convention time, Paul Patterson would begin receiving pleas from journalists who wanted to make sure they got hotel delivery of whichever *Sunpaper* would be carrying Mencken's articles. Both politicians and journalists gobbled them up.

Many also gobbled and guzzled all night at the *Sun's* traditional open suite. Mencken, who never drank at all while he still had any writing to do, usually put in only token appearances at those events. His famous capacity for food and drink was seldom tested at conventions. He was an early-to-bed, early-to-rise man. If his socializing was limited, it was also democratic. He partied with Alabama Klansmen at the 1924 Democratic convention, the most far left of the Wallace supporters at the 1948 Progressive convention. One of his noblest gestures to fairness came in 1928, when he campaigned through the dry South with wet candidate Al Smith. At a party in Nashville, *Banner* publisher James Stahlman gave all the touring reporters flasks of Tennessee corn liquor to carry with them. Mencken declined, explaining that Smith feared bad publicity if any liquor was found on his train and had asked the reporters not to risk embarrassing him. Mencken was the only reporter who turned Stahlman down.

The best tribute that I know to Mencken's convention coverage was that paid by Mark Sullivan in 1936. He wrote Frank Kent that he found Mencken's reports of the Democratic convention "the best thing I have seen in any newspaper this year, the best thing I have seen in many a year." He particularly liked Mencken's running account of the last day of the convention, an article that included descriptive details about the renominated candidates, Roosevelt and Garner, political leaders, members of the crowd, the bands. It was mostly reporting, but there was a disapproving tone throughout. Mencken had become a Roosevelt hater by then. Sullivan said he found the articles "straight and away accounts with just enough of Mencken's humor and personality to give them flavor." He suggested the *Sunpapers* enter the reports in the Pulitzer Prize contest. This was not done. Mencken dismissed the prizes as "trashy."

IX

The year 1936 was memorable for Mencken. Proposed for a Pulitzer. Offered a $1,000-a-week job. Given more assignments by the *Sunpapers* than he had had in nearly two decades. He threw himself into the political scene, attending four conventions (in addition to the major parties there were also conventions for the

32

third and fourth parties of Francis Townsend and Father Coughlin) and traveling extensively with the Republican candidate, Alf Landon. He was also helping to write and edit the *Sunpapers'* centennial history. All this work was good therapy. In 1930 he had married Sara Haardt, a teacher and writer at Baltimore's Goucher College and a regular contributor to the *Evening Sun* editorial page —and in 1935 she died. In 1933 Mencken had given up his association with the *American Mercury*. But the fuel that he drove on through most of that hectic year of 1936 often seemed to be neither the death of his wife nor the loss of his magazine, but his growing dislike of Franklin Roosevelt.

Mencken had supported FDR in 1932, reluctantly, as much out of disgust with President Hoover as anything. But by 1936 his philosophical differences with the New Deal had turned him completely against the Democrat. Mencken used to scoff at being tagged a "conservative." He said he was really a radical who preferred *no* government to even a little. The New Deal, with its centralizing of power, looked like totalitarianism to him. Further-more he had a deep personal dislike for Roosevelt that grew out of an incident in 1934. Mencken was invited to be the opposition speaker at the Gridiron Club dinner in Washington. This elite group of Washington correspondents held dinners twice a year in which the incumbent President spoke, off the record, and usually frivo-lously. The "out" party was usually represented by one of its leading officeholders. In the wake of the 1934 Congressional elections, the club's officers maintained, it was hard to find a Republican in high office. So Mencken.

Mencken appeared nervous about his chore. He hid his dislike of FDR, however, and his speech was good-natured and well received. At least some of the Gridiron members in the audience were anxious to see Mencken come off poorly. They remembered that a few years before he had run a piece in the *Mercury* that was critical of the club. They were delighted at what followed Menck-en's speech. FDR laid into him. Mencken had used the device of pretending to criticize the New Deal, then revealing at the end of his speech that he was really talking about the Anti-Saloon League. FDR used a similar device. For most of his speech, he blasted the press—but with excerpts from such Mencken essays as "Journalism in America." Mencken was furious. He formed a

33

reply in his mind, uncharacteristically a malicious one, but was not offered a chance to deliver it. As Roosevelt left the speaking area, he stopped to shake hands with Mencken. "It was fair shooting," Mencken said to him, an appraisal he repeated in his journal that night. "Despite [Roosevelt's] wide smile and his insistence that I was a friend, it was plain enough that he had a grudge and was trying to get revenge. He has had plenty of ground for wanting to do so, and he will have even more ground hereafter."

Mencken's expressions of bitterness after the event shocked some of his associates. For a while Mencken let his disgust with FDR mislead him as a journalist. In early 1936 he told one newspaper associate that if the Republicans found a better candidate than Hoover, Roosevelt could be beaten. Later Mencken was chided for saying publicly that the Republicans could beat Roosevelt with "a Chinaman." That was unfair criticism of Mencken. He had said if the Republicans could beat Roosevelt with anyone, they could beat him with that Chinaman. The point was that Roosevelt was the issue. By then Mencken no longer still believed Roosevelt could be beaten. By mid-1936 Mencken had become a friend and admirer of Landon's, but he was writing that he probably couldn't win and saying privately that he couldn't possibly win.

The *Sunpapers'* coverage of the 1936 elections was criticized for unfairness, but an interesting point about the *Evening Sun* that year was that while it refused to endorse FDR and stayed neutral on its editorial page—in part because of Mencken's arguments—it also, wholly because of Mencken's arguments, allowed Gerald Johnson to write a personal endorsement of the Democratic candidate. At the meeting at which the no-endorsement decision was made, Johnson had argued for Roosevelt and lost. As the meeting was breaking up, Mencken suggested that, since Johnson felt so strongly, he take Mencken's Monday spot on the page, instead of his usual Thursday turn, and write a "One for Roosevelt" column to balance the institutional statement of no confidence in FDR.

Mencken was back on the campaign trail in 1940 for the FDR-Wendell Willkie race. He was even more bitter about Roosevelt as war with Germany approached. But even then his enmity did not cloud his judgment as was the case with some of his colleagues. About midpoint of the campaign Mencken returned from the trail to find a "personal and confidential" message from Roy W. Howard of the Scripps-Howard chain of papers. It was a copy of a letter Howard had written another publisher, calling the then-common "Willkie can't win" stories harmful "lies." Howard wanted all the anti-FDR papers to "get on the ball" and start carrying a lot of articles stressing that Willkie was going to win. He urged Mencken to use his influence. Mencken replied in a "Dear Roy" note that the main thing wrong with the idea was that "the Willkie slump is due to Willkie's own incompetence, and there is no way known to God or man to pull him up."

X

A year into Roosevelt's second term, Hamilton Owens was promoted from the editorship of the *Evening Sun* to the more prestigious—and more conservative—*Sun*. Philip Wagner, the young journalist who was to replace him, needed a few months to learn the ropes of the editorial-page-executive routine. So Mencken was asked to take over the page for a few months. The removal of Owens, even by promotion, and the arrival of Mencken were viewed with alarm by the relatively liberal editorial writers of the afternoon paper. Though they had not been allowed to support Roosevelt, still their criticism of him was less pointed than that on the *Sun* editorial page: praise with faint damns, almost. Mencken promptly proved their fears were real. He stirred up a whirlwind—writing many bitter blasts at Roosevelt and ordering other writers to do the same. When others' editorials turned out to be less damning than the editor wanted, he would add a word or two, delete a phrase, and the result would be, in Gerald Johnson's phrase, "pure Mencken." This editing was not limited to Roosevelt editorials. Mencken edited almost everything his staff wrote.

Many of the anonymous editorials Mencken produced either by writing or editing were as full of invective as anything he ever wrote under a byline. Mencken always disliked the balanced, fair editorial. He felt people wanted to read outrageous and colorful criticism, especially when it was anonymous and seemingly institutional. Yet it is not the editorials themselves that his colleagues remember about this period. That is, it is not the content. It is the way they were written and the form they took. Mencken began writing for the February 8, 1937, edition of the paper. He wrote two editorials the first day, one the second and one the third, a pace he maintained. Each editorial appeared a day or two later. The afternoon of the 10th, to the surprise of both readers and editorial writers, the entire page consisted of one short editorial, "Object Lesson," and one million dots. Each dot stood for a federal job-holder, the editorial explained. Mencken had had the page prepared by working directly with the printers. He regularly made up the page in the composing room, so it was easy to spring the surprise on his staff.

Editorials also began to get longer and longer. Owens had preferred editorials limited to 500 words. Mencken preferred fewer and longer ones for two reasons, he told his staff. It was often easier to make a strong argument against a target in a long piece, and there were not enough important topics to justify a lot of editorials every day. (Mencken could also write short editorials when it suited his purpose. For instance, on George Washington's birthday, he wrote a one-hundred-word piece saying that the first president was "born a gentleman and remained so. . . . There have been considerable changes in the character of high American officials since the days of General Washington. . . .") The editorials got longer and longer as a rule, and early in March Mencken and Wagner turned out a combined effort that filled the entire page— with words this time, not dots. The words were bitter and bullying at times, attacking not only Roosevelt and his advisers, but also the intended beneficiaries of his government, characterized as "the one crop farmer with nothing in his head and too many children and hookworms; the city proletariat with a bad trade, or half a good one, or no trade at all; the chronic and incurable incompetent, bemused all his days by envy of his betters. Here is the real pet of the New Deal. . . ." All told, Mencken wrote thirty-six anti-New Deal editorials in three months on the job. But typically, as a concession to fairness, he allowed the maverick Johnson space for a reply to the Mencken-Wagner opus.

In some ways Mencken was a poor manager of his page and staff. He was always calling in Johnson and instructing him to get ready to do an editorial on a new subject—read up, study, leave everything else alone. A few days later, a new assignment, with the first forgotten or abandoned. He expected long hours from the staff, since he, too, was giving a lot of time to the work. But he was generous and wise in many little ways. He let the editorial writer who doubled as a drama critic come in late, on the theory that he often had to stay up late. He helped another editorial writer syndicate a light feature. And he would listen to suggestions from the writers and often let them argue him down. All this, by the way, came at the worst time of the day for Mencken, 8 A.M. or so, earlier than he liked to start working, or even thinking, when he could help it. He often came into the office (his first office job in over twenty years) in a bad humor, which made his gracious gestures all the more appreciated by a staff long since used to early rising.

Through it all, what helped keep happy the liberals on the staff was that Mencken was still Mencken when it came to individual freedoms and liberties. In the worst of his anti-New Deal editorials, he would link the Communists with Roosevelt, but he also wrote several eloquent editorials attacking legislation aimed at suppressing the rights of Communists. ("These swine have rights under our system . . ." was one ploy, but on other occasions Mencken wrote long thoughtful pleas for freedom of expression, without feeling it necessary also to disparage advocates of unpopular causes.) It was a rugged three months for all concerned. It went by fast, however; so fast, in fact, that thirty-five years later several who were on the staff then recalled that Mencken had only been their boss for one month. In May Mencken turned over the page to Wagner, and went to Johns Hopkins Hospital for a rest and diet treatment of a stomach ailment. He had also been ill with a respiratory ailment while he was editor, and he may have had the first early warnings of the strokes that would scare him the following year and cripple him within a decade.

XI

With the rise of Hitler in Germany, an old shadow fell across Mencken. Early in the decade of the '30s Mencken perceived that he was in for the same sort of troubles he had experienced during World War I, both professionally and personally. In 1933, when a

Scripps-Howard editor asked him to write a piece on Germany, he begged off, claiming it would have no market since "most of the American newspapers and magazines are violently anti-Hitler and refuse absolutely to consider his case." He never became pro-Hitler himself and before America entered the war he was ridiculing him, but he still felt Germany's policies were, for the most part, legitimate and sound. In addition to the expected charges of anti-Americanism, Mencken also became the target of charges that he was anti-Semitic. He sometimes reacted to these charges with his own bitter denunciations of "professional Jews," but he was never an anti-Semite except in the strict sense that he was "anti-everything—anti-Protestant, anti-Catholic, anti-Jewish—and, most of all, anti-bigotry," as Gerald Johnson put it. He may have been a Junker, but he was never a Nazi. As in the years before America entered World War I, Mencken wrote and said things calculated to annoy those who favored the Allied cause. He was especially angered by what he considered unfair journalism. Two weeks after war broke out in Europe, Mencken was writing in the *Sunday Sun* to complain about propaganda. He wrote a letter to an Associated Press reporter in Poland praising him for his on-the-scene coverage and deploring the fact that "most of the so-called news that is appearing in American newspapers consists of puerile speculations written in safe offices. . . . All of the prophecies in them are proved idiotic almost before they get into type." Mencken longed for the vigor to go to the war scene. But that vigor was lost, he wrote the *New York Times'* Walter Duranty in Moscow, adding, "I envy you the chance to see the show at close range."

Mencken's weekly articles for the *Sunday Sun* editorial page, which had replaced the Monday Articles, were drawing enough criticism by late 1940 to make his employers uneasy. It was growing clear that the United States would soon be in the war on the side of the British. He was mailing his most outspoken pieces to conservative publishers around the country, sometimes anonymously. And Mencken was not being prudent. When the Philadelphia *Record* asked him to comment on a number of war-related issues, his answers were like a slap in the face: Whom did he want to see win the war? He didn't care so long as it wasn't England. What did he think of his fellow brick-layer, Winston Churchill? A cheap politician of a very familiar sort who couldn't even lay bricks well. These were the views informing his writing. His old friend Paul Patterson was reluctant to ask him to tone down his writing, but when Mencken himself suggested that he stop writing the column, Patterson agreed with relief. That was in January 1941. Mencken stayed on the payroll as a consultant, though; at his own suggestion, his salary, which had risen to $12,000 a year, was reduced to $9,000. He continued to go to the *Sunpapers*' offices regularly and helped edit the new style book. He came down to the papers for the election returns in 1942, but when Patterson asked him to go to the 1944 conventions he refused.

He did not become a recluse. He still saw his friends. And, of course, he still worked every day on a supplement to *The American Language* and on his encyclopedia of quotations. His social life was little changed and, all things considered, he seemed even gay during his second exile from the pages of the *Sunpapers*. Once, in the spring of 1944, for example, he was the guest speaker at a social club at Johns Hopkins and spoke and answered questions from the youthful and enthusiastic audience till two in the morning. Visiting firemen often called on trips through Baltimore: journalists like Doris Fleeson, historians like Bell Wiley, authors, actors— people from the many worlds he had been so involved in all his life. Only journalism was closed to him and that was always the result of self-exile. In 1945 the Associated Press asked him to cover the United Nations security conference in San Francisco; not the running story, but commentary on whatever he found there to his liking. "God knows, I'd like to cover that monumental obscenity," he replied, but "all my wicked ideas and even my vocabulary are prohibited in wartime."

Conservatives were missing their Mencken, and so were liberals. At least a few were. One was Gerald Johnson. In the summer of 1944 Johnson was working in New York, pinch hitting for Lewis Gannett on the *Herald-Tribune*. He noticed in that, his first experience in New York, that many writers there often went out of their way to tell him gleefully that they knew Mencken would never come back to newspaper work after the war, that he was finished; "obviously trying to convince themselves," Johnson wrote Mencken.

"The effect on me has been to arouse an uncomfortable feeling that in Baltimore we take you too much for granted. As far as I can remember, I have never said one word to you about your withdrawal as a regular contributor to the *Sunpapers.*

"All the same, I did regret it. I understood your motives and think that perhaps you did the right thing, under the circumstances. Nevertheless, it was a blow to the papers and a loss to everyone who appreciates good writing.

"Moreover, although you may not believe it, considering how widely we differ politically, it is my belief that when the shooting is over, we are going to have on our hands a mess that only you can fumigate—if, indeed, you can. It is my pious hope, however, to live long enough to see you try. It will be tremendous . . ."

XII

Alas, it wasn't. He came back to work for the papers after the war was over, muttering that the sooner the war with the Russians started the better. He went to all three conventions in 1948—Democratic, Republican, and Henry Wallace's third party, all held in Philadelphia. At the first two he shared a suite with Westbrook Pegler; at the third, he stayed with the *Sunpapers'* regular contingent. It pleased him that he could still meet deadlines under pressure. His writing was good but not spectacular. He engaged in an argument with Wallace at one press conference, stung by a reference to "Pegler's stooges." He came home alone on the train when that last convention ended, a little concerned about a dizzy spell he had had. (He had had to leave the Republican convention early, feeling under the weather.) When the visiting condidates came to Baltimore, he covered them. One piece that drew favorable comments from his friends, and some fan mail, was his coverage of Norman Thomas' visit to Baltimore. The Socialist candidate for President met a small audience in an unglamorous, walk-up hall. Mencken, always good at descriptive writing, acquainted the readers with the scene, the number of steps up, the color of the walls, the character of the speaker, the mood of the audience. It was good Mencken, but somehow lacked a spark. Lacking that good natured ferocity that he early decided should be his hallmark, his last work could be summed up in a one-sentence answer Mencken gave to a board member who asked how the campaign was going. "It's just not the same," he sighed.

His last column appeared on November 9, 1948. It *was* bristling with a certain ferocity and that common thread that tied together all of Mencken's writings and beliefs—the libertarian's insistence that individuals should be free to do what they please if their acts do not harm others. A group of whites and blacks had played tennis together in a city park, though Baltimore's Border State personality had asserted itself by outlawing such integration. Mencken, who twenty years before had railed against the exclusion of a black poet from a banquet at a Baltimore hotel, expressed his dismay at finding "the spirit of the Georgia cracker surviving in the Maryland Free State, and under official auspices. . . . It is high time such relics of Ku Kluxery be wiped out in Maryland." Two weeks later Mencken had the serious stroke he had long feared. It left him, ironically and cruelly, able to function fairly well except that he could not read or write. He lived on in that condition for slightly over seven years. Then his heart failed, and he was celebrated again on the front pages and editorial pages of the *Sunpapers* where so much of his life's work had appeared.

XIII

Considering that Mencken, as subject, had asked that no such final journalistic send-off be given him, it would be interesting to know what Mencken the newspaperman would have had to say about those obituary issues. Whatever it was, it would have been good professional criticism. Newspapers and newspapermen were topics that Mencken wrote about often during his nearly half-century of criticism and reportage. He may have been a surer critic of newspapers than of any other facet of life. Certainly he knew that "life of kings," as he called it in his letter to Stanley Walker, as well as or better than he knew politics, literature, society, and the many other targets of his attacks. He knew newspapers from inside and from out, from top to bottom, and from horse and buggy to airplane. What follows are some of the things he had to say about his favorite calling over the years. Some are tinged with love and nostalgia, some with venom, most with wisdom, but some with wrong-headedness; all with wit, insight, and expertise. You will, I believe, find them fun to read and of more than historical pertinence.

1

Newspaper Morals

(*The Atlantic Monthly,* March 1914)

Aspiring, toward the end of my nonage, to the black robes of a dramatic critic, I took counsel with an ancient whose service went back to the days of *Our American Cousin,* asking him what qualities were chiefly demanded by the craft.

"The main idea," he told me frankly, "is to be interesting, to write a good story. All else is dross. Of course, I am not against accuracy, fairness, information, learning. If you want to read Lessing and Freytag, Hazlitt and Brunetière, go read them: they will do you no harm. It is also useful to know something about Shakespeare. But unless you can make people *read* your criticisms, you may as well shut up your shop. And the only way to make them read you is to give them something exciting."

"You suggest, then," I ventured, "a certain—ferocity?"

"I do," replied my venerable friend. "Read George Henry Lewes, and see how *he* did it—sometimes with a bladder on a string, usually with a meat-axe. Knock somebody in the head every day—if not an actor, then the author, and if not the author, then the manager. And if the play and the performance are perfect, then excoriate someone who doesn't think so—a fellow critic, a rival

43

manager, the unappreciative public. But make it hearty; make it hot! The public would rather be the butt itself than have no butt in the ring. That is Rule No. 1 of American psychology—and of English, too, but more especially of American. You must give a good show to get a crowd, and a good show means one with slaughter in it."

Destiny soon robbed me of my critical shroud, and I fell into a long succession of less aesthetic newspaper berths, from that of police reporter to that of managing editor, but always the advice of my ancient counselor kept turning over and over in my memory, and as chance offered I began to act upon it, and whenever I acted upon it I found that it worked. What is more, I found that other newspaper men acted upon it too, some of them quite consciously and frankly, and others through a veil of self-deception, more or less diaphanous. The primary aim of all of them, no less when they played the secular Iokanaan than when they played the mere newsmonger, was to please the crowd, to give a good show; and the way they set about giving that good show was by first selecting a deserving victim, and then putting him magnificently to the torture. This was their method when they were performing for their own profit only, when their one motive was to make the public read their paper; but it was still their method when they were battling bravely and unselfishly for the public good, and so discharging the highest duty of their profession. They lightened the dull days of midsummer by pursuing recreant aldermen with blood-hounds and artillery, by muckraking unsanitary milk-dealers, or by denouncing Sunday liquor-selling in suburban parks—and they fought constructive campaigns for good government in exactly the same gothic, melodramatic way. Always their first aim was to find a concrete target, to visualize their cause in some definite and defiant opponent. And always their second aim was to shell that opponent until he dropped his arms and took to ignominious flight. It was not enough to maintain and to prove; it was necessary also to pursue and overcome, to lay a specific somebody low, to give the good show aforesaid.

Does this confession of newspaper practice involve a libel upon the American people? Perhaps it does—on the theory, let us say, that the greater the truth, the greater the libel. But I doubt if any reflective newspaper man, however lofty his professional ideals, will ever deny any essential part of that truth. He knows very well that a definite limit is set, not only upon the people's capacity for grasping intellectual concepts, but also upon their capacity for grasping moral concepts. He knows that it is necessary, if he would catch and inflame them, to state his ethical syllogism in the homely terms of their habitual ethical thinking. And he knows that this is best done by dramatizing and vulgarizing it, by filling it with dynamic and emotional significance, by translating all argument for a principle into rage against a man.

In brief, he knows that it is hard for the plain people to *think* about a thing, but easy for them to *feel*. Error, to hold their attention, must be visualized as a villain, and the villain must proceed swiftly to his inevitable retribution. They can understand that process; it is simple, usual, satisfying; it squares with their primitive conception of justice as a form of revenge. The hero fires them too, but less certainly, less violently than the villain. His defect is that he offers thrills at second-hand. It is the merit of the villain, pursued publicly by a *posse comitatus,* that he makes the public breast the primary seat of heroism, that he makes every citizen a personal participant in a glorious act of justice. Wherefore it is ever the aim of the sagacious journalist to foster that sense of personal participation. The wars that he wages are always described as the people's wars, and he himself affects to be no more than their strategist and *claque.* When the victory has once been gained, true enough, he may take all the credit without a blush; but while the fight is going on he always pretends that every honest yeoman is enlisted, and he is even eager to make it appear that the yeomanry began it on their own motion, and out of the excess of their natural virtue.

I assume here, as an axiom too obvious to be argued, that the chief appeal of a newspaper, in all such holy causes, is not at all to the educated and reflective minority of citizens, but frankly to the ignorant and unreflective majority. The truth is that it would usually get a newspaper nowhere to address its exhortations to the former, for in the first place they are too few in number to make their support of much value in general engagements, and in the second place it is almost always impossible to convert them into disciplined and useful soldiers. They are too cantankerous for that, too ready with embarrassing strategy of their own. One of the principal marks of an educated man, indeed, is the fact that he does *not* take his opinions from newspapers—not, at any rate, from the militant, crusading newspapers. On the contrary, his attitude toward them is almost always one of frank cynicism, with indifference as its mildest form and contempt as its commonest. He knows that they are constantly falling into false reasoning about the things within his personal knowledge,—that is, within the narrow circle of his special education,—and so he assumes that they make the same, or even worse errors about other things, whether intellectual or moral. This assumption, it may be said at once, is quite justified by the facts.

I know of no subject, in truth, save perhaps baseball, on which the average American newspaper, even in the larger cities, discourses with unfailing sense and understanding. Whenever the public journals presume to illuminate such a matter as municipal taxation, for example, or the extension of local transportation facilities, or the punishment of public or private criminals, or the control of public-service corporations, or the revision of city charters, the chief effect of their effort is to introduce into it a host of extraneous issues, most of them wholly emotional, and so they contrive to make it unintelligible to all earnest seekers after the truth.

But it does not follow thereby that they also make it unintelligible to their special client, the man in the street. Far from it. What they actually accomplish is the exact opposite. That is to say, it is precisely by this process of transmutation and emotionalization that they bring a given problem down to the level of that man's comprehension, and what is more important, within the range of his active sympathies. He is not interested in anything that does not stir him, and he is not stirred by anything that fails to impinge upon his small stock of customary appetites and attitudes. His daily acts are ordered, not by any complex process of reasoning, but by a continuous process of very elemental feeling. He is not at all responsive to purely intellectual argument, even when its theme is his own ultimate benefit, for such argument quickly gets beyond his immediate interest and experience. But he *is* very responsive to emotional suggestion, particularly when it is crudely and violently made, and it is to this weakness that the newspapers must ever address their endeavors. In brief, they must try to arouse his horror, or indignation, or pity, or simply his lust for slaughter. Once they have done that, they have him safely by the nose. He will follow blindly until his emotion wears out. He will be ready to believe anything, however absurd, so long as he is in his state of psychic tumescence.

In the reform campaigns which periodically rock our large cities, —and our small ones, too,—the newspapers habitually make use of this fact. Such campaigns are not intellectual wars upon erroneous principles, but emotional wars upon errant men: they always revolve around the pursuit of some definite, concrete, fugitive malefactor, or group of malefactors. That is to say, they belong to popular sport rather than to the science of government; the impulse behind them is always far more orgiastic than reflective. For good government in the abstract, the people of the United States seem to have no liking, or, at all events, no passion. It is impossible to get them stirred up over it, or even to make them give serious thought to it. They seem to assume that it is a mere phantasm of theorists, a political will-o'-the-wisp, a utopian dream—wholly uninteresting, and probably full of dangers and tricks. The very discussion of it bores them unspeakably, and those papers which habitually discuss it logically and unemotionally—for example, the New York *Evening Post*—are diligently avoided by the mob. What the mob thirsts for is not good government in itself, but the merry chase of a definite exponent of bad government. The newspaper that discovers such an exponent—or, more accurately, the newspaper that discovers dramatic and overwhelming evidence against him—has all the material necessary for a reform wave of the highest emotional intensity. All that it need do is to goad the victim into a fight. Once he has formally joined the issue, the people will do the rest. They are always ready for a man-hunt, and their favorite quarry is the man of politics. If no such prey is at hand, they will turn to wealthy debauchees, to fallen Sunday-school superintendents, to money barons, to white-slave traders, to unsedulous chiefs of police. But their first choice is the boss.

In assaulting bosses, however, a newspaper must look carefully to its ammunition, and to the order and interrelation of its salvos. There is such a thing, at the start, as overshooting the mark, and the danger thereof is very serious. The people must be aroused by degrees, gently at first, and then with more and more ferocity.

They are not capable of reaching the maximum of indignation at one leap: even on the side of pure emotion they have their rigid limitations. And this, of course, is because even emotion must have a quasi-intellectual basis, because even indignation must arise out of facts. One fact at a time! If a newspaper printed the whole story of a political boss's misdeeds in a single article, that article would have scarcely any effect whatever, for it would be far too long for the average reader to read and absorb. He would never get to the end of it, and the part he actually traversed would remain muddled and distasteful in his memory. Far from arousing an emotion in him, it would arouse only *ennui*, which is the very antithesis of emotion. He cannot read more than three columns of any one subject without tiring: 6,000 words, I should say, is the extreme limit of his appetite. And the nearer he is pushed to that limit, the greater the strain upon his psychic digestion. He can absorb a single capital fact, leaping from a headline, at one colossal gulp; but he could not down a dissertation in twenty. And the first desideratum in a headline is that it deal with a single and capital fact. It must be "McGinnis Steals $1,257,867.25," not "McGinnis Lacks Ethical Sense."

Moreover, a newspaper article which presumed to tell the whole of a thrilling story in one gargantuan installment would lack the dynamic element, the quality of mystery and suspense. Even if it should achieve the miracle of arousing the reader to a high pitch of excitement, it would let him drop again next day. If he is to be kept in his frenzy long enough for it to be dangerous to the common foe, he must be led into it gradually. The newspaper in charge of the business must harrow him, tease him, promise him, hold him. It is thus that his indignation is transformed from a state of being into a state of gradual and cumulative becoming; it is thus that reform takes on the character of a hotly contested game, with the issue agreeably in doubt. And it is always as a game, of course, that the man in the street views moral endeavor. Whether its proposed victim be a political boss, a police captain, a gambler, a fugitive murderer, or a disgraced clergyman, his interest in it is almost purely a sporting interest. And the intensity of that interest, of course, depends upon the fierceness of the clash. The game is fascinating in proportion as the morally pursued puts up a stubborn defense, and in proportion as the newspaper directing the pursuit is resourceful and merciless, and in proportion as the eminence of the quarry is great and his resultant downfall spectacular. A war against a ward boss seldom attracts much attention, even in the smaller cities, for he is insignificant to begin with and an inept and cowardly fellow to end with; but the famous war upon William M. Tweed shook the whole nation, for he was a man of tremendous power, he was a brave and enterprising antagonist, and his fall carried a multitude of other men with him. Here, indeed, was sport royal, and the plain people took to it with avidity.

But once such a buccaneer is overhauled and manacled, the show is over, and the people take no further interest in reform. In place of the fallen boss, a so-called reformer has been set up. He goes into office with public opinion apparently solidly behind him: there is every promise that the improvement achieved will be lasting. But experience shows that it seldom is. Reform does not last. The reformer quickly loses his public. His usual fate, indeed, is to become the pet butt and aversion of his public. The very mob that put him into office chases him out of office. And after all, there is nothing very astonishing about this change of front, which is really far less a change of front than it seems. The mob has been fed, for weeks preceding the reformer's elevation, upon the blood of big and little bosses; it has acquired a taste for their chase, and for the chase in general. Now, of a sudden, it is deprived of that stimulating sport. The old bosses are in retreat; there are yet no new bosses to belabor and pursue; the newspapers which elected the reformer are busily apologizing for his amateurish errors,—a dull and dispiriting business. No wonder it now becomes possible for the old bosses, acting through their inevitable friends on the respectable side,—the "solid" business men, the takers of favors, the underwriters of political enterprise, and the newspapers influenced by these pious fellows,—to start the rabble against the reformer. The trick is quite as easy as that but lately done. The rabble wants a good show, a game, a victim: it doesn't care who that victim may be. How easy to convince it that the reformer is a scoundrel himself, that he is as bad as any of the old bosses, that he ought to go to the block for high crimes and misdemeanors! It never had any actual love for him, or even any faith in him; his election was a mere incident of the chase of his predecessor. No wonder that it falls upon him eagerly, butchering him to make a new holiday!

This is what has happened over and over again in every large

49

American city—Chicago, New York, St. Louis, Cincinnati, Pittsburgh, New Orleans, Baltimore, San Francisco, St. Paul, Kansas City. Every one of these places has had its melodramatic reform campaigns and its inevitable reactions. The people have leaped to the overthrow of bosses, and then wearied of the ensuing tedium. A perfectly typical slipping back, to be matched in a dozen other cities, is going on in Philadelphia today. Mayor Rudolph Blankenberg, a veteran warhorse of reform, came into office through the downfall of the old bosses, a catastrophe for which he had labored and agitated for more than thirty years. But now the old bosses are getting their revenge by telling the people that he is a violent and villainous boss himself. Certain newspapers are helping them; they have concealed but powerful support among financiers and business men; volunteers have even come forward from other cities— for example, the Mayor of Baltimore, himself a triumphant ringster. Slowly but surely this insidious campaign is making itself felt; the common people show signs of yearning for another *auto-da-fé*. Mayor Blankenberg, unless I am the worst prophet unhung, will meet with an overwhelming defeat in 1915. And it will be a very difficult thing to put even a half-decent man in his place: the victory of the bosses will be so nearly complete that they will be under no necessity of offering compromises. Employing a favorite device of political humor, they may select a harmless blank cartridge, a respectable numskull, what is commonly called a perfumer. But the chances are that they will select a frank ringster, and that the people will elect him with cheers.

Such is the ebb and flow of emotion in the popular heart—or perhaps, if we would be more accurate, the popular liver. It does not constitute an intelligible system of morality, for morality, at bottom, is not at all an instinctive matter, but a purely intellectual matter: its essence is the control of impulse by an ideational process, the subordination of the immediate desire to the distant aim. But such as it is, it is the only system of morality that the emotional majority is capable of comprehending and practicing; and so the newspapers, which deal with majorities quite as frankly as politicians deal with them, have to admit it into their own system. That is to say, they cannot accomplish anything by talking down to the public from a moral plane higher than its own: they must take careful account of its habitual ways of thinking, its moral thirsts and prejudices, its well-defined limitations. They must remember clearly, as judges and lawyers have to remember it, that the morality subscribed to by that public is far from the stern and arctic morality of professors of the science. On the contrary, it is a mellower and more human thing; it has room for the antithetical emotions of sympathy and scorn; it makes no effort to separate the criminal from his crime. The higher moralities, running up to that of Puritans and archbishops, allow no weight to custom, to general reputation, to temptation; they hold it to be no defense of a ballot-box stuffer, for example, that he had scores of accomplices and that he is kind to his little children. But the popular morality regards such a defense as sound and apposite; it is perfectly willing to convert a trial on a specific charge into a trial on a general charge. And in giving judgment it is always ready to let feeling triumph over every idea of abstract justice; and very often that feeling has its origin and support, not in matters actually in evidence, but in impressions wholly extraneous and irrelevant.

Hence the need of a careful and wary approach in all newspaper crusades, particularly on the political side. On the one hand, as I have said, the astute journalist must remember the public's incapacity for taking in more than one thing at a time, and on the other hand, he must remember its disposition to be swayed by mere feeling, and its habit of founding that feeling upon general and indefinite impressions. Reduced to a rule of everyday practice, this means that the campaign against a given malefactor must begin a good while before the capital accusation—that is, the accusation upon which a verdict of guilty is sought—is formally brought forward. There must be a shelling of the fortress before the assault; suspicion must precede indignation. If this preliminary work is neglected or ineptly performed, the result is apt to be a collapse of the campaign. The public is not ready to switch from confidence to doubt on the instant; if its general attitude toward a man is sympathetic, that sympathy is likely to survive even a very vigorous attack. The accomplished mob-master lays his course accordingly. His first aim is to arouse suspicion, to break down the presumption of innocence—supposing, of course, that he finds it to exist. He knows that he must plant a seed, and tend it long and lovingly, before he may pluck his dragon-flower. He knows that all storms of emotion, however suddenly they may seem to come up, have their origin over the rim of consciousness, and that their gathering is really a slow, slow business. I mix the figures shamelessly, as mob-masters mix their brews!

It is this persistence of an attitude which gives a certain degree of immunity to all newcomers in office, even in the fact of sharp and resourceful assault. For example, a new president. The majority in favor of him on Inauguration Day is usually overwhelming, no matter how small his plurality in the November preceding, for common self-respect demands that the people magnify his virtues: to deny them would be a confession of national failure, a destructive criticism of the Republic. And that benignant disposition commonly survives until his first year in office is more than half gone. The public prejudice is wholly on his side: his critics find it difficult to arouse any indignation against him, even when the offenses they lay to him are in violation of the fundamental axioms of popular morality. This explains why it was that Mr. Wilson was so little damaged by the charge of federal interference in the Diggs-Caminetti case—a charge well supported by the evidence brought forward, and involving a serious violation of popular notions of virtue. And this explains, too, why he survived the oratorical pilgrimages of his Secretary of State at a time of serious international difficulty—pilgrimages apparently undertaken with his approval, and hence at his political risk and cost. The people were still in favor of him, and so he was not brought to irate and drumhead judgment. No roar of indignation arose to the heavens. The opposition newspapers, with sure instinct, felt the irresistible force of public opinion on his side, and so they ceased their clamor very quickly.

But it is just such a slow accumulation of pin-pricks, each apparently harmless in itself, that finally draws blood; it is by just such a leisurely and insidious process that the presumption of innocence is destroyed, and a hospitality to suspicion created. The campaign against Governor Sulzer in New York offers a classic example of this process in operation, with very skillful gentlemen, journalistic and political, in control of it. The charges on which Governor Sulzer was finally brought to impeachment were not launched at him out of a clear sky, nor while the primary presumption in his favor remained unshaken. Not at all. They were launched at a carefully selected and critical moment—at the end, to wit, of a long and well-managed series of minor attacks. The

52

fortress of his popularity was bombarded a long while before it was assaulted. He was pursued with insinuations and innuendoes; various persons, more or less dubious, were led to make various charges, more or less vague, against him; the managers of the campaign sought to poison the plain people with doubts, misunderstandings, suspicions. This effort, so diligently made, was highly successful; and so the capital charges, when they were brought forward at last, had the effect of confirmations, of corroborations, of proofs. But, if Tammany had made them during the first few months of Governor Sulzer's term, while all doubts were yet in his favor, it would have got only scornful laughter for its pains. The ground had to be prepared; the public mind had to be put into training.

The end of my space is near, and I find that I have written of popular morality very copiously, and of newspaper morality very little. But, as I have said before, the one is the other. The newspaper must adapt its pleading to its clients' moral limitations, just as the trial lawyer must adapt *his* pleading to the jury's limitations. Neither may like the job, but both must face it to gain a larger end. And that end, I believe, is a worthy one in the newspaper's case quite as often as in the lawyer's, and perhaps far oftener. The art of leading the vulgar, in itself, does no discredit to its practitioner. Lincoln practiced it unashamed, and so did Webster, Clay, and Henry. What is more, these men practiced it with frank allowance for the naïveté of the people they presumed to lead. It was Lincoln's chief source of strength, indeed, that he had a homely way with him, that he could reduce complex problems to the simple terms of popular theory and emotion, that he did not ask little fishes to think and act like whales. This is the manner in which the newspapers do their work, and in the long run, I am convinced, they accomplish far more good than harm thereby. Dishonesty, of course, is not unknown among them: we have newspapers in this land which apply a truly devilish technical skill to the achievement of unsound and unworthy ends. But not as many of them as perfectionists usually allege. Taking one with another, they strive in the right direction. They realize the massive fact that the plain people, for all their poverty of wit, cannot be fooled forever. They have a healthy fear of that heathen rage which so often serves their uses.

Look back a generation or two. Consider the history of our

democracy since the Civil War. Our most serious problems, it must be plain, have been solved orgiastically, and to the tune of deafening newspaper urging and clamor. Men have been washed into office on waves of emotion, and washed out again in the same manner. Measures and policies have been determined by indignation far more often than by cold reason. But is the net result evil? Is there even any permanent damage from those debauches of sentiment in which the newspapers have acted insincerely, unintelligently, with no thought save for the show itself? I doubt it. The effect of their long and melodramatic chase of bosses is an undoubted improvement in our whole governmental method. The boss of today is not an envied first citizen, but a criminal constantly on trial. He is debarred himself from all public offices of honor, and his control over other public officers grows less and less. Elections are no longer boldly stolen; the humblest citizen may go to the polls in safety and cast his vote honestly; the machine grows less dangerous year by year; perhaps it is already less dangerous than a *camorra* of utopian and dehumanized reformers would be. We begin to develop an official morality which actually rises above our private morality. Bribetakers are sent to jail by the votes of jurymen who give presents in their daily business, and are not above beating the street-car company.

And so, too, in narrower fields. The white-slave agitation of a year or so ago was ludicrously extravagant and emotional, but its net effect is a better conscience, a new alertness. The newspapers discharged broadsides of 12-inch guns to bring down a flock of buzzards—but they brought down the buzzards. They have libeled and lynched the police—but the police are the better for it. They have represented salicylic acid as an elder brother to bichloride of mercury—but we are poisoned less than we used to be. They have lifted the plain people to frenzies of senseless terror over drinking-cups and neighbors with coughs—but the death-rate from tuberculosis declines. They have railroaded men to prison, denying them all their common rights—but fewer malefactors escape today than yesterday.

The way of ethical progress is not straight. It describes, to risk a mathematical pun, a sort of drunken hyperbola. But if we thus move onward and upward by leaps and bounces, it is certainly better than not moving at all. Each time, perhaps, we slip back, but each time we stop at a higher level.

2

The Public Prints

(*The Smart Set*, July 1918)

I

Of all the literate arts and crafts journalism seems to have the most meagre literature; even writing for the moving-pictures, though it is still in diapers, can show twice as many textbooks and treatises. There is not even a presentable history of the American newspaper, for the late Frederic Hudson's work, which is excellent so far as it goes, stops with the year 1872, and the newspaper, it must be plain, has passed through more changes since that time than during the four centuries preceding. As for technical books, laying down the principles and practise of the editorial rooms, they are both very scarce and very bad. Nearly all of them are the product, not of active newspaper men who know what they are talking about, but of fly-blown editorial writers turned into professors of journalism, or of theorizing *Privatdozenten* in remote and highly Baptist "universities." Back in the nineteenth century, as a young reporter ambitious to shine, I studied *Steps Into Journalism,* by Edwin L. Shuman, then of the Chicago *Tribune.* It was feeble enough stuff, God knows, and I got very little out of it, but to this day it remains the best book in its field. Not all the bombastic faculties of all the schools of journalism, posturing before the chautauquas in their doctoral gowns, have put forth anything better, nor even anything so good.

Why newspaper men write so little about their own profession is a problem that has often puzzled me. The notion that they haven't the time is nonsensical, for they are forever writing books on other subjects. It is, indeed, hard to find an American journalist above the rank of police reporter who hasn't written at least one book. Nor is it a fact that there is no public for professional treatises. On the contrary, the few that exist are very widely read, and even if actual newspaper men disdained them there would still be a large sale for them among the innumerable youngsters who aspire to journalistic careers. The true cause of the dearth, I suspect, lies in the fact that the gentlemen of the press, as a class, are an unreflective and unanalytical lot—that they seldom give any sober thought to the anatomy and physiology of the business of their lives. That business, indeed, holds them by its very conditions in a state of mind which is the opposite of the analytical. They enter upon it romantically, and when the romance is gone they go along wearily and unthinkingly. It is a trade that uses men up, especially mentally. That is to say, it is a trade that makes them stupid. The old journalist, allowing everything for his gigantic accumulation of useless knowledge, is nine times out of ten an ignorant and muddle-headed fellow, unfit for anything save keeping to his rut. His mind is a storehouse of ancient (and usually inaccurate) labels and rubber stamps. To think anything out for himself, clearly and vigorously, is quite beyond him.

Part of the blame for this mental deadening falls upon the unescapable conditions of the craft. It makes such heavy demands upon the wits, it insists upon so high a degree of aliveness, that it is no wonder that, once the bounce of youth is gone, a man begins to rely upon formulae. To be forty years old and the city editor, say, of an afternoon paper is almost as impossible as to be sixty years old and a star base-runner. The only way for a man in that boat to navigate it at all is for him to transform himself into a sort of automatic machine—that is, to throw overboard reflection and trust to mere reaction. He simply cannot think fast enough for the job; it asks for a younger man, still full of gas and folly, still bare of caution and conscience. In brief, the whole thing is a young man's adventure, like marrying or going to war. Once youth has been used up, and with it its resilience, there ensues a fossilization exactly like that which all the world notes in elderly military gentlemen and in men long broken to marriage. The typical newspaper man of discreet years may be likened to an unfortunate who married his best girl at twenty-one and has lived through disillusionment and disgust and a wondering self-searching, and has finally taken refuge behind a fear to think about it at all.

So much for what is inherent, and probably unavoidable. The way out, perhaps, is to retire at thirty, or to slide a razor across the carotids at forty. But on top of this there are influences quite outside the man himself, and even outside the legitimate constitution of the craft. Those influences, I believe, are a good deal more complex than they are ordinarily made out to be. It is common to describe them by saying, simply, that the editorial room is now in bondage to the business office—that newspapers are now run, not to propagate ideas, but to make money. But that is neither quite accurate, nor quite the whole story. The trouble with the newspapers of America, taking one with another, is not that they are run fundamentally to make money, but that they are run by men who already have money, and want something else. And the trouble with the working newspaper man is not that the business office attacks him by frontal assault and tyranny, but that he is destroyed by an infinitely subtle sapping and mining. In all other professions a man's security grows greater as he gains in age and experience. In journalism alone his position grows more precarious. Thus menaced from above by powers and purposes that are at odds with his professional pride and integrity, and that he often cannot even understand, and from below by a younger generation that presses harder every day, it is no wonder that he commonly degenerates into a timorous and platitudinous fellow, his thoughts more and more concentrated upon mere self-preservation, and the fine frenzies and gallantries of his youth swallowed up by a hollow capacity for whatever is cheap, and easy, and safe.

Well, what is to be done about it? I'm sure I don't know. I merely describe a disease; I do not propose a remedy. One of the primary difficulties lies in the fact that entrance into journalism is almost as facile as entrance into jail. No equipment is required— not even a sound education. Nine-tenths of the recruits who come in, of course, turn out to be incompetents, but it is precisely the pressure of these incompetents that makes the man above insecure. Perhaps the schools of journalism, now flourishing so prodigiously, will raise the existing standards a bit, if only by making actual literacy a requirement. But I doubt it. All they will probably accomplish will be to make the younger generation more surefooted and hence more exigent. Nor do I see any way to get the control of newspapers out of the hands of the devious fellows who now gobble them one by one. A rich man wants to get on in politics, or he seeks a way to protect his business, or he has social ambitions, or he is moved by some vague yearning to exert power and be somebody. Well, he has the money and it is a free country. What are you going to do about it? The answer lies in the plain facts. You are not going to do anything about it. It is happening every day. In every large American city at least half (and sometimes all) of the newspapers are now owned and dominated by men who have other interests, and whose other interests are a great deal more tender and precious in their sight than the business of telling what has happened in the world, fairly and completely, and of interpreting it frankly and fearlessly.

II

All of which leads me, blowing my nose sadly, to two late tomes: *The Profession of Journalism,* by a herd of journalists under command of Prof. Dr. Willard Grosvenor Bleyer, a gifted pedagogue of Wisconsin (Atlantic Monthly Press), and *Northcliffe: Britain's Man of Power,* by William E. Carson (Dodge). The latter is a highly flattering and even oleaginous work: Dr. Carson depicts Northcliffe as one of the most praiseworthy of existing mammals. This business, of course, involves a certain amount of soft pedalling. The atrocious badness of most of the Northcliffe publications is scarcely mentioned, nor is there any detailed and accurate account of the noble lord's adventures in politics, particularly before the war. But the book, nevertheless, is instructive and worth reading, for it obviously depicts Northcliffe very much as he sees himself, and there is high entertainment in gazing into the recesses of so gargantuan and puissant a personality. The man is almost archaic in his might and daring—a medieval baron come to life again. I often see him compared to Hearst, especially by his enemies. As well compare the Matterhorn to a load of cinders. He is, in fact, equal to a whole drove of Hearsts. Nor is Roosevelt his peer, nor any other American I can think of. He is, in fact, the sole creature of his species in Christendom today; no other private individual has a hundredth of his power. And how did he get it? He got it by printing magazines and newspapers of the most imbecile type, and by circulating them in the fashion of Barnum and Munyon. He got it by playing cynically and magnificently upon the stupidity and emotionability of the least intelligent—by pulling the public ear. . . . What the moral is, God knows!

The Profession of Journalism, as I say, is a composite. Various journalists and pseudo-journalists discuss the thing, chiefly lugubriously—among them, Rollo Ogden, Oswald Garrison Villard, Melville E. Stone, Henry Watterson, Francis E. Leupp and two or three anonymous blabbers. I myself have a chapter in the book, and following it there is a counterblast to it by Ralph Pulitzer, of the New York *World.* Diligently studying this counterblast for the second time—it first appeared, like my chapter, in the *Atlantic Monthly* during 1914—I am set in my conviction that I made my allegations, not too gaudy, but too mild. All I can find in my discourse is a platitude—to wit, that the grand moral frenzy of newspapers is chiefly buncombe—that their true motive, nine times out of ten, is not to purge the republic of sin, but merely to give a hot show, stir up the animals, and so make circulation.

The truth is that this crusading business is one of the worst curses of journalism, and perhaps the main enemy of that fairness and accuracy and intelligent purpose which should mark the self-respecting newspaper. It trades upon one of the sorriest weaknesses of man—the desire to see the other fellow jump. It is at the heart of that Puritanical frenzy, that obscene psychic sadism, which is our national vice. No newspaper, carrying on a crusade against a man, ever does it fairly and decently; not many of them even make the pretense. On the contrary, they always do it extravagantly and cruelly, pursuing him with dishonest innuendo, denying him his day in court, seeking to intimidate his friends. The practise, I believe, is disastrous to newspapers, and to newspaper men. The fact that they fight behind breastworks, against an enemy who can't strike back, makes poltroons of them. That sort of thing is not war; it is lynching—and lynching is surely no sport for men presumably of honor. In particular, the effects are evil when the men told off for the enterprise do not believe in it, which is much oftener than the public imagines.

I speak here, not as a moralist preaching an impossible ethic, but as one who has engaged in such doings at length, and without hypocritical regrets. I was once employed, in fact, as a specialist in invective by a newspaper proprietor who had formidable enemies to dispose of, and I naturally augmented the stock company of victims by adding a few persons whom I disliked myself. But when I get to hell I shall be at least able to file two caveats against my incineration—one that I signed my name to every line I wrote, and was physically and financially responsible for all stretchers, and the other that I gave every aggrieved man, absolutely without condition, full liberty to strike back in my own paper, at any length and in any terms. These counterblasts often filled double the space of my own fancies. Moreover, they had just as much display. Yet more, they were printed promptly. The result was a combat that kept a certain plain fairness, even when it was most violent. Nobody was stabbed in the back. Nobody was denied his day in court. Sometimes I got the better of it, and sometimes I got a good pummelling. The gallery was pleased in both cases.

A banal story, to be sure. What is the point? The point is that, so far as I know, there is not a single newspaper in the whole United States today that offers any such fair play to its opponents—that not a single one of them, to the best of my knowledge and belief, has a fixed rule, publicly known and invariable, allowing an aggrieved man to state his defense in his own terms. I say "in his own terms." What I mean especially is in terms of countercharge. Such a rule, if general in America, would expose and ruin literally scores of newspapers. And some of them would be big ones, and influential ones, and vociferously virtuous ones.

3

On Journalism

(*The Smart Set*, April 1920)

I

Upton Sinclair's long anticipated philippic against the reptile press of our great Wesleyan republic, now published at last under the somewhat fanciful title of *The Brass Check,* runs true to Socialist form in two salient ways. That is to say, it is full of a moral indignation that is undiluted by the slightest smear, trace or homeopathic attenuation of humor, and it winds up with a remedy that is simple, clear, bold and idiotic.

That remedy I need not describe with too much particularity; it has been set forth in *The Nation, The Appeal to Reason* and other forward-looking gazettes by Dr. Sinclair himself, and no doubt *The Profiteer's Review* and other such organs of reaction have given it copious critical notice. In its essence it contemplates raising a fund of $1,3000,000, founding a weekly to be devoted to "the truth, the whole truth and nothing but the truth," and then appointing a committee of master-minds to determine just what the truth is. This last device, in the secrecy of my cabinet, gives me a lot of malicious joy. Dr. Sinclair's nominations to the committee give me even more. Think of Samuel Untermyer, Amos Pinchot and Frank A. Vanderlip sitting down in solemn state to dispose of the problem that stumped and flabbergasted the great Graeco-Roman intellect of Pontius Pilate! Imagine a board of examiners of the latest Woodrovian tosh made up of Charles Edward Russell, Herbert Croly and Allan Benson, all eager witnesses to the immutable truth of the tosh of yesteryear! And fancy Max Eastman, Rabbi Stephen S. Wise and Mrs. J. Borden Harriman told off to inquire into the merits of the latest shindig in Ireland, or of the presidential platform of General Dr. Leonard Wood, or of the next set of Sisson documents, by the editor of *Comic Cuts* out of the American Historical Association! More charming still, try to picture the plain people throwing the Hearst papers, the *World* and the *Evening Telegram* into the ash-barrel, and then waiting patiently for six days for the *National News* (the proposed name of the Sinclair *zeitung*) to tell them the plain and unvarnished truth, unrelieved by the slightest aesthetic exaggeration!

And what of the raw material? How are these drum-head courts of eminent gnosiologists to arrive at their judgments? Where is the evidence coming from? Let Dr. Sinclair answer. "When the Centralia incident occurs," he says, "you telegraph to a professor in the University of Washington to proceed immediately to Centralia, at the paper's expense, and to telegraph one thousand words about what actually happened in the riot." What could be simpler? Welcome an old, old friend: the theory of the divine inspiration of the *Privat Dozent*. One glance, and the learned man grasps all the facts that Chambers of Commerce, Rotary Clubs, American Legions, patriotic Mayors, Department of Justice perjurers, Federal judges with eyes higher up, and lying newspaper reporters have labored abominably to conceal. And then, his thousand words on the wire, he goes back to his university—and is at once knocked in the head by his 100 per cent American trustees. . . .

Thus Sinclair, the incurable romantic, wholesale believer in the obviously not so. The man delights me constantly. His faith in the wisdom of the incurably imbecile, the virtue of the congenitally dishonest, the lofty idealism of the incorrigibly sordid is genuinely affecting. I know of no one in all this vast paradise of credulity who gives a steadier and more heroic credit to the intrinsically preposterous. But that is as far as I care to go in contumely of him. Allowing everything for his lack of humor, his chronic moral indignation, his strangely distorted will-to-believe, his hypertrophied trust in God, it must be plain to every competent observer that in *The Brass Check* he has achieved a very interesting piece of writing, a picaresque chronicle of a high order, and that the things he sets forth as facts are, in the majority of instances, undeniably true. The newspapers will denounce him as a liar debauched with Bolshevik money, the generality of laymen will suspect him of gross exaggeration, and he may find himself, in the end, with some nasty damage suits on his hands. But if my testimony is worth anything under American rules of evidence (*e.g.*, that the deduction of a government detective is worth more than the sworn statement of an eye-witness, that every man who reads an I. W. W. leaflet may be presumed to be plotting to overthrow the Constitution by force, and that it is a proof of guilt for an accused man to send for a lawyer and demand to be confronted by his accusers), then I offer it in his cause most cheerfully. I have been in almost constant practise as a journalist since the year 1899. I have held every editorial job that newspapers have to offer, from that of dramatic critic to that of editor-in-chief. More, I have no old grudges in my gizzard. I was always paid as much as I was worth. I was never discharged, no one ever charged me with being an idealist, and I am at this moment on the best of terms with every newspaper that I have ever had anything to do with. What I desire to say is simply this: that to the best of my knowledge and belief, the average American newspaper, even of the so-called better sort, it not only quite as bad as Dr. Sinclair says it is, but ten times worse —ten times as ignorant, ten times as unfair and tyrannical, ten times as complaisant and pusillanimous, and ten times as devious, hypocritical, disingenuous, deceitful, pharisaical, pecksniffian, fraudulent, knavish, slippery, unscrupulous, perfidious, lewd and dishonest. . . .

Alas, alas! I understate it horribly! The *average* American newspaper, *especially* of the so-called better sort, has the intelligence of a Baptist evangelist, the courage of a rat, the fairness of a Prohibitionist boob-bumper, the information of a high-school janitor, the taste of a designer of celluloid valentines, and the honor of a police-station lawyer. Ask me to name so many as five papers that are clearly above this average—challenge me to nominate five that are run as intelligently, as fairly, as courageously, as decently and as honestly as the average nail factory, or building and loan association, or Bismarck herring importing business—and I'll be two or three days making up the list. And when I have made it up and the names are read by the bailiff, a wave of snickers will pass over the assembly after nearly every one. These snickers will come from newspaper men who know a shade more about the matter than I do.

II

What ails the newspapers of the United States primarily—and what ails Dr. Sinclair's scheme of reform quite as plainly—is the fact that their gigantic commerical development compels them to appeal to larger and larger masses of undifferentiated men, and that the truth is a commodity that the masses of undifferentiated men cannot be induced to buy. The causes thereof lie deep down in the psychology of the *Homo boobus,* or inferior man—which is to say, of the normal, the typical, the dominant citizen of a democratic society. This man, despite a superficial appearance of intelligence, is really quite incapable of anything properly describable as reasoning. The ideas that fill his head are formulated, not by a process of ratiocination, but by a process of mere emotion. He has, like all the other higher mammalia, very intense feelings, but, like them again, he has very little genuine sense. What pleases him most in the department of ideas, and hence what is most likely to strike him as true, is simply whatever gratifies his prevailing yearnings—for example, the yearning for physical security, that for mental tranquillity and that for regular and plentiful subsistence. In other words, the thing he asks of ideas is precisely the thing he asks of institutions, to wit, escape from doubt and danger, freedom from what Nietzsche called the hazards of the labyrinth, above all, relief from *fear*—the basic emotion of all inferior creatures at all times and everywhere. Therefore this man is generally religious, for the sort of religion he knows is simply a vast scheme to relieve him from a vain and painful struggle with the mysteries of the universe. And therefore he is a democrat, for democracy is a scheme to safeguard him against exploitation by his superiors in strength and sagacity. And therefore, in all his miscellaneous reactions to ideas, he embraces invariably those that are the simplest, the least unfamiliar, the most comfortable—those that fit in most readily with his fundamental emotions, and so make the least demands upon his intellectual agility, resolution and resourcefulness. In sum, he is an ass.

The problem before a modern newspaper, hard pressed by the need of carrying on a thoroughly wholesome business, is that of enlisting the interest of this inferior man, and by interest, of course, I do not mean his mere listless attention, but his active emotional cooperation. Unless a newspaper can manage to arouse his *feelings* it might just as well not have at him at all, for his feelings are the essential part of him, and it is out of them that he dredges up his obscure loyalties and aversions. Well, and how are his feelings to be stirred up? At bottom, the business is quite simple. First scare him—and then reassure him. First get him into a panic with a bugaboo—and then go to the rescue, gallantly and uproariously, with a stuffed club to lay it. First fake him—and then fake him again. This, in substance, is the whole theory and practise of the art of journalism in These States. In so far as our public gazettes have any serious business at all, it is the business of snouting out and exhibiting new and startling horrors, atrocities, impending calamities, tyrannies, villainies, enormities, mortal perils, jeopardies, outrages, catastrophes—first snouting out and exhibiting them, and then magnificently circumventing and disposing of them. The first part is very easy. It is almost unheard of for the mob to disbelieve in a new bugaboo. Immediately the hideous form is unveiled it begins to quake and cry out: the reservoir of its primary fears is always ready to run over. And the second part is not much more difficult. The one thing demanded of the remedy is that it be simple, more or less familiar, easy to comprehend—that it make no draft upon the higher cerebral centers—that it avoid leading the shy and delicate intelligence of the mob into strange and hence painful fields of speculation. All healthy journalism in America—healthy in the sense that it flourishes spontaneously and needs no outside aid—is based firmly upon just such an invention and scotching of bugaboos. And so is all politics. And so is all religion. Whatever stands above that fundamental imposture is an artificiality—a plaything of men with more hopes than sense. Intelligent and honest journalism, intelligent and honest politics, even intelligent and honest religion—these things, in a democratic

65

society, have no legitimate place. They are, when they are encountered, exotic curiosities, pale and clammy orchids, half-fabulous beasts in cages. Take away the steam heat, the milk bottle, the hypodermic, and poof! they are gone.

III

Thus it seems to me to be rather an injustice, and far too facilely smug and moral, to blame the low state of the public prints in the nation upon the rascality of their owners and conductors. The trade of printing them, of course, is evil, and so the men who are attracted to it are chiefly evil, too, but the primary evilness is not in the trade or the traders but in the customers. In this department much senseless gabble goes on against such fellows as Hearst. I do not know this Hearst, have never witnessed him in the flesh, and have never worked for any of his newspapers or magazines, but when I observe him being denounced piously by other journalists it always makes me laugh. The men who principally attack him are not actually his superiors as moralists; they are simply his inferiors as practical journalists—and uncomfortably conscious of it. At the height of the recent crusade against him they made a deliberate effort to dispose of him in the manner made classical by his own gazettes. That is to say, they deliberately lied about him. The theory behind this strategy was quite plain. They hoped to embarrass him doubly—first by taking advantage of the public's axiomatic willingness to believe in bugaboos, and secondly by jockeying him into the difficult position of having to tell the truth in his defense. This second handicap was heavier than the first: it would have been sufficient to have finished a less skillful journalist. But Hearst was a better man than his enemies; he was better singly than all of them taken together. Instead of wasting time upon a defense that would have injured him in proportion as it was dignified and honest, he simply devoted his whole talents to inventing bugaboos more horrible than any the opposition was parading in his image, and soon the crowd turned willingly to his better show, and the opposition began to wabble, and then to go to pieces. Hearst came out of the battle with one of the best bugaboos ever broken to harness, to wit, the English bugaboo. If, before another year goes groaning by, he doesn't scare the plain people half to death with it, then I overestimate his talents and miss my guess.

As I say, much pishposh is talked about the alleged difference between yellow journals and more respectable journals. The difference is precisely that between a bootlegger and a Sunday-school superintendent, which is to say, nothing. It is my honest belief, based upon twenty years of close observation and incessant reflection, that the odds, if any, are mainly in favor of the yellow journals. Taking one day with another, they are probably less malignantly mendacious. The things they lie about are largely things of no possible importance—divorce suits, petty grafts, the buffooneries of society, the doings of chorus girls. In such fields, I'd just as lief read a lie as the truth: it is usually, in fact, more amusing. But in the domain of politics, government and high finance the yellow journals probably get a good deal closer to the truth than the more austere journals, nine-tenths of which are owned by men who are engaged in some sort of exploitation of the boobery. I do not say that the yellow journals make any actual effort to be exact; on the contrary, they make a palpable effort to avoid a too literal exactness. But when they go on alleging, day after day, that every politician is a scoundrel and that every public service corporation is run by swindlers and that all the operations of Wall Street have the one aim of shaking down the plain people, they get near enough to the truth for any practical purpose. They have to dramatize and fictionize that truth to make it go down. It must be made improbable in order to convince the plain people. But this, at worst, is mere shopman's exaggeration, well defended by the legal maxim of *caveat emptor.* The lying of the more respectable papers is less innocent. Its aim is not merely to sell extras to simple folk; its aim is to perpetrate a deliberate fraud upon them, to the profit of gentlemen who remain behind the scenes.

IV

The owners of yellow journals, in fact, are the only genuine journalists left in the country. They are commonly cynical men, with a shrewd understanding of the intellectual limitations of the proletariat, but most of them have no ulterior motive in alarming and bamboozling it—their whole profit comes from the unspeakable balderdash they empty upon it. The trouble with the newspapers higher up the scale is that nearly all of them are now owned by men who regard journalism as no more than a handmaiden to some larger and more profitable enterprise—as a convenient means to the befuddling and anaesthetizing of a public that would otherwise be against them—as it actually is whenever the yellow journals turn upon them and expose them. The precise nature of that larger and more profitable enterprise is not always obvious. It is easy, of course, to put two and two together when a wealthy contractor, or land grabber, or bank manipulator buys a newspaper, or when one is bought by a man notoriously eager for high public office. But now and then the buyer is a fellow whose business is more or less reputable and who shows no yearning to sit in the Senate. What of him? Why does he hazard so much money on such a gamble? The answer is to be found very often, I believe, in his unadorned *Wille zur Macht*—his quite human desire to be an important and powerful man in his community, to be courted by all the local schemers and magnificoes, to dictate legislation, to make and unmake officeholders, to pull the glittering wires of politics. And sometimes, I suspect, his ambition (or, perhaps more accurately, his wife's) is merely social. He wants to dine in certain houses, to languish at certain haughty dances—above all, to have certain guests at his shiny new house on Gold Hill. Well, a man who controls an important newspaper has no difficulty about achieving these things. The keys of scandal are in his pocket. He is powerful. He can reward and punish, directly and indirectly. The hopes of all other men within his jurisdiction are in his keeping. Imagine him able to remember that the lemonade in the finger-bowl is not to be drunk, and he can get into society if he wants to.

Whatever the underlying motive or motives, the fact remains that the newspapers of the United States are fast passing out of the hands of professional journalists and into the hands of men who are primarily something else. Every issue of the weeklies devoted to journalistic gossip prints news of another important transaction of that sort. The transfers of the *Evening Post* from Oswald G. Villard to one of the Morgan partners and of the Bennett papers to

Munsey were not isolated phenomena; they were quite typical of a general and rapidly progressive tendency. And even when no Munsey or Morgan partner appears openly, it is common for the thing to happen behind the door. One hears first that some old-time editor-proprietor has died or gone bankrupt, one hears secondly that his paper has been bought for $2,000,000 cash by some right-thinking journalist notoriously unable to pay a poker debt of $29, and one hears thirdly, in discreet whispers, that the real buyer is old John Googan, the eminent sheet-asphalt contractor, or Irving Rosehill, president of Rosenberg, Cohen & Co., the patriotic banking firm, or the illustrious Senator Lucius Snodgrass, oil operator, leading Methodist layman and perpetual candidate for the embassy at St. James'. Not long ago, when Iceberg Fairbanks died and autopsy was had upon his remains, it was discovered that he had owned the leading newspaper of Indiana for years. Most of them cover it up more carefully; even the coroner is fooled. But the men who work upon a newspaper so held in pawn know pretty well what to avoid. There is in nearly every newspaper office a certain Awful Name. It precedes that of God.

On such a newspaper—that is, on the normal, the typical American newspaper—it must be obvious that the quest for truth, the whole truth and nothing but the truth is commonly mitigated by something not unlike policy. On the one hand, the staff has to make a paper that will sell, and is thus forced to keep the mob stirred up with the traditional buncombe, and on the other hand it has to avoid stepping on the large, numerous and exquisitely sensitive toes of the Googan, or Rosehill, or Snodgrass in the background. (In my early days he was a wealthy ice-magnate, and every story that he was interested in, say nine or ten a night, went to the composing room marked "Ice ! !") It needs no long argument to convince the judicious that the business of moulding public opinion under such conditions tends to slacken a working journalist's hold upon the concept of truth, and, in the end, upon the concept of honor. Engaged day in and day out in propagating ideas that he knows to be untrue and idiotic, and forced to make himself an instrument of enterprises that he sometimes cannot understand and must often regard as sinister, he ends by losing all sense of public responsibility, and so becomes a mere kept blackguard, ready at the word of command to defend the guilty or to harass and

69

persecute the innocent. In the end a very fury of malignancy possesses him. The power is in his hands and the conscience is gone. He is simply an eighth-rate man with the capacity for evil of a Napoleon—and chronically running amok. This epidemic destruction of the ordinary decency of the journalist is responsible for many of the things complained of by Dr. Sinclair in his book—the bitter and relentless pursuit of victims, the gross contempt of common honesty, the utter disappearance of the habits of courtesy and fairness prevailing among civilized men. A paper so polluted becomes a public menace. Its word is worth nothing. It carries on its jehads maliciously, unintelligently and cravenly. It denies all hearing to its prey. An appeal to its honor is as vain as an appeal to the honor of a Congressman.

Such newspapers, as I say, tend to become inordinately numerous. There was a time, say twenty years ago, when they were still exceptional; today they are the rule, and, in some parts of the country, amost the invariable rule. Do not misunderstand me! I am not protesting against mere exaggerated zeal—the laudable desire of a journalist to please his boss. I am not, in fact, protesting against anything. I am simply *describing* something, not even in sorrow, but simply as a specialist in human depravity. What I want to make clear is the fact that such newspapers are deliberately and utterly dishonest—that they carry on their entertaining and harrowing of the mob without the slightest regard for the ordinary decencies. And what I want to make plain also is the fact that they are fast driving out all other sorts of journals. Such a paper, with power in its hands, is quite without any regard for the rights of individuals. Let a man fall a victim to its mendacity, and he is devoid of any reasonable redress. His statement of his case is distorted or suppressed. His defenders are scared off. And if, despairing of fair play, he appeals to the courts, he finds very quickly that the courts in nearly all the larger American cities fear the newspapers with a holy fear, and that the man who wins a libel action *and gets his money* is quite as rare as the man who bites a lion and lives to tell the tale.

I shall be here accused, I daresay, of dirty talk against my old trade, and in particular of dirty talk against its hardworking practitioners. But the facts are the facts. That trade has undergone a ghastly metamorphosis during the past few decades. There was a time when the actual boss of nearly every important newspaper was a practical newspaper man, with professional pride in his work, some notion of his public responsibility, and usually an honorable reputation within the craft, at least locally. To the young reporter this fellow was an idol. His journalistic theories were cherished and quoted, his style was imitated, every youngster on the staff hoped to follow in his footsteps. But today the actual boss of a newspaper tends more and more to become a shadowy figure in the background, ignorant of newspaper traditions and ways of thinking, and heavily engaged in enterprises that have a way of colliding harshly with what remain of newspaper ideals. This man is beyond the journalistic circle; no young reporter dreams of stepping into his shoes some day; any ambition to be like him must needs involve abandoning journalism as a trade forthwith. The first result is that the trade itself ceases to be charming; it is no longer a romantic co-operation of free equals, but a form of labor like working in a rolling-mill, with unionism offering the only feasible means of keeping it even bearable. And the second result is that the sort of men who formerly entered upon its practise with a high sense of its dignity are now turned into other courses, and that the typical recruit of today is a tacky and eighth-rate fellow, with no more capacity for professional self-respect than a garbage-man.

I suspect that the late Joseph Pulitzer had his eye on this tendency when he set up his School of Journalism. There are now many such schools, but I doubt that they accomplish much. On the one hand, they all seem to be falling into the hands of professional pedagogues—a class already ground down into the mire by a plutocratic tyranny even worse than that which oppresses journalism. And, on the other hand, the most a school of journalism can hope to accomplish, even supposing it to inculcate a civilized code of ethics, is to breed young reporters who will escape from journalism with their hands clasping their noses immediately they become privy to the inner workings of a typical newspaper office. Those that stick will be either stupid fellows who do not notice the bad air, or spineless fellows who get used to breathing it, or raffish fellows who like it. I glance at random through a magazine devoted to the entertainment and instruction of working newspaper men. The first article that my eye alights upon is an elaborate description, by a man employed by various well-known papers, of his private methods of manufacturing news. One of the news items, thus manufactured, that he points to with pride involved introducing the name of a real woman, presumably respectable, into a grotesque, idiotic and utterly lying story. I pass on. The second article to attract me embodies an invitation to reporters to write lively accounts of their encounters with women who have given them scandalous stories unwittingly—the wives of criminals approached by subterfuge, women complainants in divorce cases, and so on. I turn to another such magazine. It prints a long article describing how certain Washington correspondents of important papers, admitted to the press galleries of Congress in that character, act as "press agents for interests concerned in legislation," are "engaged in propaganda work of one kind or another," are "openly or secretly employed by political parties and politicians," and have been guilty of "serious violations of the confidence of State, War and Navy officials."

The allegations last quoted aroused a good deal of discussion in journalistic circles. But what was done in the end? So far as I have been able to discover, absolutely nothing. The men described are still working for newspapers, and engaged in their other activities on the side. Some, I daresay, also hold political jobs—a favorite means of promoting the honor of journalism. Well, why not? It is surely not *infra dig.* for a reporter to act as a "press agent for interests concerned in legislation"; he is probably already a direct employe of "interests concerned in legislation." And why shouldn't he be "engaged in propaganda work of one kind or another"; isn't his paper already engaged in "propaganda work" of far more than one kind or another? And wherein lies the discredit in being "openly or secretly employed by political parties and politicians" when the boss is running for the Senate, and employing the paper to convince everyone that his opponents are all thieves, and loading its heaviest guns to fight off all inquiry into the expenditure of his campaign fund?

4

A Gang of Pecksniffs

(Baltimore *Evening Sun,* May 2, 1922)

I

On the first page of the eminent *Sunpaper* of last Friday appeared a dispatch from New York reporting that the American Newspaper Publishers' Association, there assembled for its annual convention and booze-guzzle, had passed a solemn resolution protesting that "the liberty of the press has been seriously threatened during the past year," pledging its members to "resist all interference with the right . . . of the press to free expression under the constitutional guarantees," and instructing its Committee on Federal Laws "to exercise its utmost efforts to maintain the liberty of freedom (sic) of the press wherever it may be threatened." On the same page of the *Sunpaper,* two columns away, appeared a dispatch from Philadelphia reporting that two women had been arrested and jailed for "distributing circulars which petition President Harding to grant amnesty to political prisoners."

Humor? Then the obscene is humorous—as, indeed, most normal Americans seem to hold. As for me, I see nothing to cackle over in the resolution of the publishers. Instead, it should be denounced briefly for what it is: a mass of degraded and disgusting cant. In the history of American journalism during the past half dozen years there is certainly nothing jocose. In all their dealings with the question of free speech the newspapers of the country, and especially the larger and more powerful ones, have been infinitely pusillanimous, groveling, dishonest and indecent. If, as they now pretend so boldly, their editors and proprietors are actually in favor of Article I of the Bill of Rights, then their long acquiescence in its violation proves that they are a herd of poltroons. And if, when it was so grossly violated, they were actually in favor of those who violated it, then their belated resolution proves that they are liars. I see no way to avoid these alternatives. I can imagine no process of reasoning, however subtle and ingenious, whereby persons whose words and acts are so heroically at odds could be converted into honest and honorable men.

II

It is my private impression, born of long familiarity with such fauna, that what brought most of the publishers to the side of the Bill of Rights at last, after all their craven consenting to its invasion, was not any belated enthusiasm for free speech, or, indeed, any intelligent respect for it or understanding of it, but simply and solely a fear that the next violation of Article I would probably cut off some of their revenues. The uplifters are up and doing on all sides, and of late they have uncovered some Great Causes that threaten newspaper profits. For example, there is the matter of race-track information. Practically all American newspapers, however moral they may seem on their editorial pages, print such information on their sporting pages—and it sells a good many papers. Now the uplifters propose a Federal law declaring any paper containing it unmailable. At once, waking from their long sleep, the publishers begin shedding crocodile tears over "the right of the press to free expression under the constitution guarantees"!

It would be difficult to imagine any more gross and obvious pecksniffery. Put beside it, the proceedings of the Anti-Saloon League seem almost honest. Where were all these publishers when the janissaries of the late Woodrow were prowling the country, clubbing and jailing all citizens who presumed to question his divinity—when men by the hundred were railroaded to prison for

74

venturing to exercise their constitutional right to free speech, and other men were harassed and hounded in a dozen other ways, and publications almost without number were tyrannically barred from the mails? The answer is simple: they were not only consenting to the business; they were actively promoting it. It was their newspapers—many of them great and puissant papers—that egged on the Department of Justice, the Chambers of Commerce, the Americanization Leagues, the American Legion and all other such lawless bands. It was their newspapers that raised the idiotic alarm about Bolshevism, and brought on the wholesale jailing and deportation of innocent men. It was their newspapers that distorted and tortured the news to official uses, and debauched the courts, and connived at crime, and made justice in America a joke. And it was their newspapers that fawningly approved every time some smaller and more honorable sheet got into trouble for trying to tell the truth.

III

I am well aware, of course, that there were exceptional journals that shrunk delicately from much of this swinery—that a few of them came forward with protests long before the race-track information bill alarmed the rank and file. I say a few, but at the moment I am sure of but two: the estimable *Sunpaper* aforesaid and the New York *World*. The *World* was the first to gag, and then came the *Sunpaper*. By the time the Palmer buffoonery about radicals got to its height, both were in full revolt, and trying to tell the truth. But it is not to be forgotten that even these very exceptional and almost miraculous gazettes ran a long way behind some of the weeklies and monthlies—that they were magnificently silent at the times the *Masses* was suppressed and the *Nation* was attacked. In brief, they deserve very little praise for their revolt, for by the time they came to make it it was quite safe. When they were needed most desperately—when the aid of two such rich and powerful papers would have been most effective and valuable— they were silent. To have horned in at that time would have been to run grave risks, for Wilson was strutting about in his halo and Palmer and company believed themselves invincible—but it would have been to render a public service of inestimable worth. I believed at that time and I believe now that in a stand-up fight with Wilson they would have won—that public opinion, after the first clash, would have supported them, as it later came to support even the *Masses*. But instead of making the venture they went to the defense of Wilson, and it was not until he was on his knees that they began to gag at his excesses, and, in particular, at his deliberate, cynical and intolerable violations of the Bill of Rights.

Even then they tried ineptly to separate the man from his evil deeds, e.g., to argue that the cad who kept the poor old ass, Debs, in prison was a statesman and a gentleman. Worse, they continued to pussyfoot, even after they had got over that folly. For example, they denounced the crimes against the Constitution perpetrated by the Ku Klux Klan, and were silent. about the far more serious crimes perpetrated by the American Legion. But, even so, they were a million times more honest and courageous than any other American newspapers. It was at least obvious that something resembling a conscience had begun to gnaw them. The rest of the great American journals continued to display, as usual, the morals and public spirit of so many Prohibition enforcement officers, Congressmen, or streetwalkers.

IV

These preposterous fakes now begin to snuffle and blubber over the invasion of the Bill of Rights! Hit in the money-bag, they suddenly become fanatical devotees of the Constitution! It is my sincere hope that even Congressmen will have sense enough to penetrate the fraud. To more intelligent and seemly men I offer a ready test of it. Get a copy of any great American journal of Friday, April 28, 1922. See how its news department treated the story from Philadelphia—of the two women dragged to the cala-boose by the police for exercising their constitutional right to petition the President for the release of men jailed in violation of *their* constitutional rights. Then see what the staff Delane has to say about the business on the editorial page—if anything. Don't bother to read his learned discourse on the Genoa mountebankery, the sins of the coal miners, the candidacy of M. Cox. Go straight to his denunciation of this double assault upon the Constitution—if it is there. If you find it, let me know.

5

Max Ways as H. L. Mencken Knew Him

(Baltimore *Evening Sun*, June 5, 1923)

Max Ways, I dare say, will be remembered by most Baltimoreans as a politician, but to those of us who served with him on the old *Morning Herald*—now dead, alas, for 17 years!—he will always remain the perfect model of the city editor. City editing is surely no trade for indolent or for fussy men. . . . It is bad enough today, with a new and vast mechanical equipment for the handling of news and a harsh, military discipline prevailing in daily journalism; it was far worse in the last years of the old century, with the telephone scarcely developed beyond a toy, and no taxicabs or aeroplanes for use in a pinch, and the whole corps of journalists infected by the delusion that they were literary gents and artists, and hence not amenable to the regulations governing messenger boys and counter-jumpers.

Max got himself together a staff of strange fish, indeed, and managed to manufacture with their aid—often, indeed, in spite of them and against their violent opposition—the liveliest morning newspaper ever seen in these parts. This was accomplished partly by the sheer magic of an extraordinarily charming personality; he had a way with him that could get honest work out of even the most bacchanalian old reporter. But more important than this charm was the force of his hard professional competence. He had been a reporter himself and a very good one, and he knew every dodge

77

and backwater of the trade. No one could fool him; no one could leave a job half done and escape his withering denunciation. His vocabulary, in those days, had a florid effulgence, well suited to the exigencies of his office. I have seen him reduce a veteran court reporter almost to tears by a few ferocious blasts; more, I have seen him swear down and silence the foreman of the composing room, an achievement almost superhuman.

But it was not only by such assaults that he got his work done: it was far more often by shrewd advice and delicate flattery. When I was 20 years old I worked for him 12 hours a day, often seven days a week, for the wage of $14.00. Some weeks I averaged 5,000 words of copy a day—an inconceivable stint for a modern reporter. But it was not hard work; it was going to school—and in a school infinitely agreeable and romantic. He read every line of copy himself, and just as he never missed an inaccuracy, a banality, a rubber-stamp phrase, so he never missed anything that had any merit in it. Nor was he silent about what he discovered. The whole office knew it instantly—sometimes with the effect of making a young reporter wither to the size of one of the office cockroaches, and sometimes with the effect of making him walk on air.

Max was the only city editor I ever heard of who had no enemies on his own staff. They slaved for him, often with violent murmurs, but they always loved him, and, what is much more, respected him. He knew his trade thoroughly, and every man under him was aware of it. He knew how to handle a big story economically and quickly; he knew how to detect and offset schemes to "work" the paper; above all, he knew and esteemed good journalistic writing. I well remember the first private palaver I ever had with him, a greenhorn just in from the street. "I don't expect you," he said, "to beat *The Sun* boys getting the bald news. The *Sunpaper* has the people of Baltimore in its pocket. If it doesn't send a man for the news, they send it in themselves. The best you can do in that department is to match them evenly. But if you can't beat them *writing* the news after you have got it, then all I can say is that you are a —— —— —— —— —— ——."

A pity that such a man ever left journalism. He gave it color and charm. When he threw away his editorial pencil and took to politics, something very genuine was lost. He was a thoroughly competent editor, and an incomparably likable man.

6

Watterson's Editorials Reveal "Vacuity of Journalism"

(A review of *The Editorials of Henry Watterson*,
compiled with an introduction and notes
by Arthur Krock. Baltimore *Evening Sun*,
August 11, 1923)

This is an extremely depressing book. For 40 years or more Watterson was the most distinguished editorial writer on the American press, quoted endlessly and known everywhere, and yet in this large volume of his best editorials, very intelligently and fairly selected by his chief-of-staff, Mr. Krock, there is scarcely a line that is worth rereading today. What ailed Watterson, of course, was that he was pre-eminently the professional editorial writer, engaged endlessly upon a laborious and furious discussion of transient futilities.

During all the while that he wrote upon politics—and no man ever wrote more copiously or to greater immediate applause—he was apparently wholly unconscious of the underlying political currents of the country. The things he discussed were simply the puerile combats of parties and candidates; politics, to him, was scarcely to be distinguished from a mere combat for job. On all other subjects he was equally hollow and superficial—for example, on prohibition, which he attacked violently without understanding it, and without the slightest apparent realization of its certainty of triumph. His editorials on foreign politics are empty mouthings of an unintelligent chauvinism. His occasional ventures into economics are pathetic.

Why editorial writing in the United States should be in such low estate is hard to understand. It enlists a great deal of excellent writing ability—Watterson himself, indeed, was an extremely charming writer—and, whatever it was in the past, it is now relatively free. Nevertheless, the massed editorial writers of the United States seldom produce a new idea, and are almost unheard of when the problems of the country are soberly discussed. Of all the writers who have published important and influential books upon public affairs during the past decade, not one, so far as I can recall, was a newspaper editorial writer, and not one owed anything to editorial writers for either his facts or his arguments. One might naturally suppose that men devoted professionally to the daily discussion of public questions would frequently achieve novel and persuasive ideas about them, and be tempted to set forth those ideas in connected and effective form, but the fact remains that nothing of the sort ever happens.

What is printed in the newspapers of the United States, acres and acres of it every day, is dead the day after it is printed. Nine-tenths of it is mere babble and buncombe, and the rest seems to lack, somehow, the elements that make for conviction and permanence. The newspapers do not lead in the formation of public opinion; they either follow the mob or feebly imitate a small group of leaders. In Watterson's book I can't recall reading a single sensible thing that had not been said, before he said it, by some one else.

Perhaps the anonymity of editorial writing is largely to blame for its flaccidity. The lay view is that anonymity makes for a sort of brutal vigor—that the unsigned editorial is likely to be more frank and scathing than the signed article. But the truth is quite the opposite. The man who has to take personal responsibility for what he writes is far more apt than the anonymous man to be frank. He cannot hedge and evade the facts as he sees them without exposing himself to attack and ridicule. He must be wary and alert at all times, and that very circumstance gradually strengthens him in his opinions, and causes him to maintain them tenaciously and with vigor.

Under the cover of anonymity it is fatally easy to be facile and lazy—to take refuge behind the prevailing platitudes. The anonymous writer gets no personal credit for it when he is intelligent, fair and eloquent; there is thus a constant temptation upon him to lighten his labors by employing formulae. Even Watterson, who was known by name to all of his readers, often succumbed to this temptation, for his actual editorials were unsigned, and when he was idiotic his admirers charitably blamed it upon his subordinates. Writing steadily over his own name, I am convinced that he would have done far better work. As it is, Mr. Krock's collection can be regarded only as an appalling proof of the general vacuity of American journalism. It is the most awful exposure of an editorial writer since the publication of Dr. Fabian Franklin's "People and Problems."

7

The Newspaper Man

(A review of *The Principles of Journalism,* by Casper S. Yost,
and *The Ethics of Journalism,* by Nelson Antrim Crawford.
The American Mercury, June 1924)

Mr. Yost, a man of sixty, has been editor of the editorial page of
the St. Louis *Globe-Democrat* since 1915, and is the author of three
books, a treatise entitled *A Successful Husband,* a report on the
buffooneries of *Patience Worth,* and a history of the late war. Mr.
Crawford, a man of thirty-six, is professor of industrial journalism,
whatever that may be, at the Kansas State Agricultural College, a
thirty-second degree Mason, a member of the Manhattan, Kansas,
Rotary Club, and the editor of an anthology called *Weavers With
Words.* Their books are much alike in plan, and both might have
had the same title; Mr. Yost, indeed, uses Mr. Crawford's title as
one of his chapter headings. Perhaps a still better title for both
would have been one used by Miss Jane Addams thirteen years ago
in another but not unrelated connection: "A New Conscience and
an Ancient Evil." For what both gentlemen deal with is the current
stirring of ethical discontent and soul-searching within the journalistic craft—the faint, feeble beginnings of the notion that newspaper editors ought to be men of honor, or, at all events, that they
ought to subscribe to the theory that it would be somehow nice if
they *were* men of honor. This notion is a relative novelty. When I
began my apprenticeship in journalism, twenty-five years ago, it

82

was cherished only by a very small minority of journalists, and most of them cherished it in blushful secrecy, as they cherished their literary ambitions. To the average journalist of that time the craft was not a profession at all, but a game, and its code was indistinguishable from that of poker or craps. It was unethical to do in a colleague by false pretenses, but everything else, apparently, was ethical. Those were the palmy days of reporters who hid in chimneys and purloined papers, of city editors who were let in on good things, and of managing editors who enjoyed political sinecures. The public position of a journalist was above that of a streetwalker but below that of a police captain.

In late years there has been some change—not much, perhaps, but surely some. It has been mainly brought about, I believe, not by practicing journalists themselves, but by the men most of them hate bitterly, to wit, the grasping capitalists who have gradually engulfed two-thirds of the principal American newspapers. All the surviving deficiencies of journalism among us are laid at the door of these Babbitts in Greeley whiskers, or at the door of the advertisers they are supposed to fear and obey, but the plain and unescapable truth is that journalism under their hoof is at least ten times as decent and dignified as it was when it was supposed to be free, and that working for them, to a journalist of self-respect, is at least ten times as agreeable as working for the cheap, blackmailing, incompetent and trivial gazettes of the Golden Age. The difference, roughly, is that between a bank and a one-ring circus. The bank may be dull and promotion in it may be slow, but it at least demands that its employes shall wash behind the ears and snitch no petty cash; the one-ring circus expects them to sleep with the horses and to make up the shortage in their wages by picking pockets. The old-time newspapers were seldom honest, and almost never intelligent. Was even the New York *Herald* intelligent? I doubt it gravely. The *Herald* was the richest newspaper in America a generation ago, and yet it underpaid its men, it knocked them about as brutally as if they had been Reds accused of reading the Constitution, and it reflected editorially the ethics and ideas of a man who, for practically all his adult life, found it safer and more comfortable to live outside the United States. The *Herald* was one of the best; the worst were sorry indeed. The typical American newspaper of the time was not rich but needy—and needy newspapers, like needy men, can't afford to be squeamish. Three-fourths

83

of the journals of the land would print anything in their advertising columns that was paid for and could get through the mails, and fully two-thirds of them would throw in some *lagniappe* in their editorial and news columns. They were ignorant, partisan, corrupt and puerile, and most of the men who owned them were for sale.

I believe that the gradual absorption and amalgamation of our newspapers by men of large means—the substitution of Munseys, Hearsts, Scrippses and Curtises for the old-time dodgers and shysters—has greatly elevated the standards of American journalism. For all these *entrepreneurs,* save only Hearst, I must confess that I have little professional respect. Munsey seems to me to be a dreadful dullard, and Curtis is a mere manufacturer. Nevertheless, both have the high merit, at least, that they are not for sale; both are able to pay for what they want; more important still, both *know* what they want. The editorial writer who works for them may not enjoy propagating their stale ideas, but he may at any rate console himself with the reflection that those ideas remain relatively stable —that they cannot be changed overnight by an advertising contract or a political job. In other words, the entrance of such opulent vacuums into the field has accomplished a reform that was almost unthinkable under the old regime: it has made newspapers genuinely independent—and independence, even when it is ignorant, is obviously a thousand times as a respectable as the old cadging and groveling. When orders come down from Munsey or Curtis the man who gets them, though he may regard them as ill-advised, is at least in no doubt about their honesty. He may execute them without any feeling that they make him the instrument of dishonorable motives. He is not condemned to acts whose true purposes he would not dare to put into words, even to himself. His predecessor, I believe, enjoyed no such consolation. The reporter or editor of a generation ago seldom had any illusion about the *bona fides* of his boss. It took a powerful sentimentality to make him believe in his paper, and not infrequently even sentimentality was impotent without the aid of ethyl alcohol.

The major trouble with journalism today, I am convinced, is that the men of the craft have not sufficiently grasped the change that is going on under their noses—that they still think mainly in terms of the journalism of the last century. Journalism as a business, in brief, has grown faster than journalism as a profession. Too many of the old-timers still linger in editorial rooms, and their influence tends to preserve the skullduggery and incompetence that should have been got rid of long ago. They find it a sheer impossibility to lift themselves to a professional level; they are still slaves, and they look and act the part. They still belong to press clubs (*i.e.,* organizations designed to induce ward politicians, bootleggers and city contractors to pay the rent on the theory that contact with journalists will benefit them), they still take a childish pride in a puerile Philistinism, and they are still far too willing to do anything they are ordered to do, absolutely without challenge. I doubt that many orders subversive of sound journalistic practice come from the owners who are now blamed for everything; most of them are too ignorant of journalism to know all its darkest backalleys. Such malpractices are ordained by superiors within the craft, or arise out of the journalist's own lack of professional dignity and conscience. No rich owner, I believe, ever ordered his slaves to print deliberate lies about Russia, or to write bad English day in and day out, or to maul and make nonsense of every human concern above the comprehension and tastes of a bartender. No advertiser ever demanded that political mountebanks be treated with solemn gravity, or that the funeral of a Harding be described in the language of a Methodist revival, or that helpless men, with the mob against them, be pursued without sense, decency or fairness. The blame for such offenses rests upon newspaper men, not upon their masters. As professional men, they will continue to sit below the salt until they consider soberly the present low state of their craft and take measures to renovate it.

The books of Mr. Yost and Prof. Crawford represent first efforts to effect that renovation. Both seek to formulate codes of ethics for the practicing journalist. Their methods of approach differ considerably. Mr. Yost, an editorial writer of long experience, seems to be quite unable to get beyond the blowsy platitudinousness of his order. What he says is mainly obvious, and a great deal of it, like most things that are obvious, is also untrue. He seems, indeed, to be almost if not quite devoid of ideas. Mr. Crawford, a younger and better informed man, is much more original and intelligent. He sees clearly that the fundamental journalistic problem is a problem in mob psychology, and he discusses it with considerable shrewdness and not too much pious pretense. He lacks the authority of Mr. Yost, but he also lacks the dullness.

8

The Reporter at Work

(A review of *The Best News Stories of 1923*, edited by Joseph Anthony.
The American Mercury, August 1924)

Just what Mr. Anthony's qualifications may be for deciding what is good, what is better and what is best in current journalism I don't know. *Who's Who in America* is silent about him, and his introduction to his collection reveals nothing save a familiarity with a few threadbare journalistic platitudes. But the collection itself, barring the hollow bombast of the title, seems to me to be extremely interesting, and even somewhat instructive. For what it offers is a very fair cross-section of American journalistic writing—not the best, perhaps as genuinely competent judges of narrative English would choose the best, but certainly a reasonable approximation to what would be looked upon with pride in the average newspaper office. The job of the reporter, obviously, differs considerably from that of the writer on more lofty planes. He not only does his work against time, with no opportunity to devise the "spontaneous" ornaments of style that spring out of second thought; he must also bear in mind that he is writing for an audience that, in the main, is no more than barely literate, and so keep himself within the bounds of its narrow information and elemental taste. Worst of all, he must write stuff that will commend itself to his immediate superiors, the copy-readers—men chosen, more often than not, because they are efficient rubber-stamps rather than because they are competent judges of English style. The result of these various pressures is that the sagacious reporter, whatever his natural urge to originality, inevitably takes refuge in *clichés*. They save him trouble doubly—first the trouble of devising something better, and secondly the trouble of having the copy-desk down on him. When he writes according to the mode he both pleases his immediate superiors and delights the customers of his newspaper.

The effects of these forces are plainly visible in many of the news stories reprinted by Mr. Anthony. For example, turn to one from the Philadelphia *Inquirer* by Hugh Harley: a report of a jail delivery from the Eastern Penitentiary. The thing happened at 10.25 P.M., and it is highly probable that midnight was striking before Mr. Harley had gathered the facts and was back in the *Inquirer* office, ready to write his story. He made a very competent job of it, setting forth all the essential circumstances clearly and even getting a certain dramatic power into it. But he could accomplish the business only by falling back upon the *clichés* that a young reporter learns almost as soon as he learns how to make out an expense account. In his first sentence one discovers that the escape was "sensational"; in his second that one of the three men who got away was caught "after a chase of several blocks"; in his third that the other two "are still at liberty." In paragraph two one encounters "dash for freedom"; in paragraph four a clubbed guard "summons his waning strength" and has "blood streaming" from his wounds; in paragraph seven the adjacent householders are "terrorized"; in subsequent paragraphs the pursuing cops "scour" the neighborhood, the prison guards are ordered to "shoot to kill," the fleeing prisoners "elude their vigilance," an extra-watchful guard is "met by a fusillade of bullets," another rushes from his cage "to learn the cause of the disturbance," and "it is the work of a moment" for the convicts to open the prison gate. Meanwhile, a police lieutenant "calls every available policeman to his aid," citizens join in the "man hunt," the news "spreads like wildfire," alarmed housewives leap into the street "carrying tiny infants in their arms," and the "break for liberty" is pronounced "the most daring ever conceived."

I here attempt no sneer at Mr. Harley. His story was plainly written under circumstances that would have reduced a Walter Pater or a James Branch Cabell to a despairing thumb-sucking. Nevertheless, it is yet fair to point out that, as a specimen of narrative English, it is very flabby and obvious stuff—that its effects are all traditional set pieces, familiar from long use. It is a statement of fact in a stale and often half meaningless jargon; as literature it simply has no existence. The same thing is true of at least four-fifths of the news stories in Mr. Anthony's book—most of them, I believe, submitted by editors as among the best things printed by their papers during 1923. In only a small minority of these stories, even those written more leisurely, is there any genuine distinction of style, any actual feeling for words, any sense of the superb plasticity and resilience of the English language; in even fewer is there any noticeable originality of thought. The reporter thinks as he writes: in well-worn patterns. His view of the world, as he grows up in the trade, becomes increasingly Philistine; when the wide-eyed wonder of the first year or two oozes out of him its place is taken by a facile and unintelligent cynicism, with room for bathos in it. One finds him, in this book, growing maudlin over the death of Harding, who "passed with the sunset"; one sees him stirred by the same heroics that stir baseball umpires, sophomores and office boys. The world he inhabits is one in which Rotary Club orators are taken seriously, the Bolsheviki are "bloodthirsty wild beasts," and visiting intellectuals say that "in every Russian child's heart, no matter of what class, there is love for America!"

But perhaps I generalize too freely. A few extraordinary reporters seem to survive, somehow, the crippling strain of the city room, even the bellicose imbecility of the copy-readers. In the present book I encounter, here and there, some strangely intelligent stuff. I point, for example, to a story by Louis Weizenkorn in the New York *World*: it might have been at home in the *Sun* of twenty-five years ago, before Munsey's dreadful presence laid the ghost of Dana. And to one by Harry T. Brundidge from the St. Louis *Star*. And to one by Paul Y. Anderson from the St. Louis *Post-Dispatch*. And to one by Julian Sargent from the St. Paul *Pioneer-Press*. There are others, too. But not many.

9

Memoirs of an Editor

(A review of *Memoirs of an Editor,* by Edward P. Mitchell.
This appeared under another title in
The American Mercury, December 1924)

Permit me, gents, an exultation and a sentimentality. Reading, the other evening, Mr. Mitchell's charming volume, I came, on page 381, to a few words that sent a thrill through me from glabella to astragalus. The editor of the New York *Tribune* is thrilled no more when he gets a picture postcard from H. M. King George, nor King George when he beats the chaplain of Windsor at parcheesi. And what caused all this uproar in my recesses? Simply the bald mention of my name—a line and a half of pleasant politeness—by the editor of the old New York *Sun.* I doubt that I can make you understand it. For you were not, I take it, a hopeful young newspaper reporter in the year '99, and so your daily food and drink, your pastor and your bootlegger, your dream and your despair, was not the *Sun.* Dana was dead then, but Munsey had not yet come in to make a stable of the shrine. The reigning editor was Edward P. Mitchell—scarcely a name to the barbarians without the gates, but almost a god to every young journalist. I would not have swapped a word from him, in those days, for three cheers from the Twelve Apostles. He was to me the superlative journalist of this great, heroic land, as the *Sun* itself was the grandest, gaudiest newspaper that ever went to press. I have suffered much from heartache and heartburn in the twenty-five years that have passed since then, and in consequence my store of wisdom has increased so vastly that my knees begin to buckle under it, but I still believe that my judgment of Mitchell and the *Sun* was sound, and I herewith ratify and reiterate it in the solemnest tones I can muster. The one is retired now, and puts in his mornings communing with Habakkuk, his prize turkey-gobbler, and in watching the deer come out of his woods; the other is a corpse hideously daubed to make it look like a respectable groceryman with fashionable aspirations. This Republic will be luckier than it deserves if it ever looks upon their like again.

The dull professors who write literary histories never mention the New York *Sun.* It is not even listed in the index to the Cambridge History of American Literature, though the Baltimore *American* and the New York *Staats-Zeitung* are both there! Nevertheless, I presume to believe that its influence upon the development of American literature, and particularly upon the liberation of the younger writers of its time from the so-called American tradition, was incomparably greater than that of any of the magnificos hymned in the books. What Dana and his aides taught these youngsters was double: to see and savor the life that swarmed under their noses, and to depict it vividly and with good humor. Nothing could have been at greater odds with the American tradition. The heroes of the Stone Age were all headed in other directions. The life of their place and time interested them very little, especially the common, the ordinary life, and depicting things vividly was always far less their purpose than discussing them profoundly. Even Holmes and Walt Whitman, despite their superficial revolts, ran true to type: they were philosophers long before they were artists. The only exceptions were the humorists, and all the humorists were below the salt: even Mark Twain had to wait until 1910, when death was upon him, before the first American of any literary authority accepted him ungrudgingly. It was the great service of Dana that he stood against all this mumbo-jumbo. From its first issue under his hands the *Sun* showed a keen and unflagging interest in the everyday life of the American people —in the lowly traffic of the streets and tenements, in the tricks and devices of politicians and other zanies, in all the writhings and cavortings of the national spirit. And it depicted these things, not in a remote and superior manner, but intimately and sympathetically, and with good humor and sound understanding. To Dana such a man as Big Tim Sullivan was not a mere monster, to be put in a barrel of alcohol and labeled "Criminal"; he was, above all, a human being—imperfect, perhaps, but still not without his perfections. And so, at the other end, were the communal heroes and demigods. Dana saw through all the Roosevelts, Wilsons and Coolidges of his time; they never deceived him for an instant. But neither did they outrage him and set him to spluttering; he had at them, not with the crude clubs and cleavers of his fellows, but with the rapier of wit and the bladder of humor. Long before *Main Street* he had discovered the street itself, and peopled it with a rich stock company of comedians. And long before *Babbitt* he had paved the way for all the "Babbitts" that remain to be written.

Mr. Mitchell notes with some surprise that the *Sun,* at least in its earlier days, was not read by the Best People—that it was barred, for example, from the reading-room of the Century Club. I see nothing surprising in that. The Century Club, then as now, was a gloomy sarcophagus of petrified brains; its typical member was a man of immense dignity and no intelligence. The *Sun,* to the end of the Dana-Mitchell-Laffan dynasty, was never popular among such dull pedants; not until Dr. Munsey added it to his chain of journalistic grocery-stores did they begin to read it. Even today it seems to be little esteemed by the decayed editorial writers and unsuccessful reporters who teach in schools of journalism; so recently as last month I was urging them to make more use of its files. Such stupid fellows, when they were in practice, did not admire the *Sun;* they admired the New York *Times,* the Cincinnati *Enquirer* and the Washington *Post.* But the *Sun* had plenty of other customers, and many of them were converted into disciples. It was at the hands of these men, I believe, that American literature was delivered from its old formalism and hollowness. They were the young reporters who made the movement of the nineties. They became the novelists, the dramatists and the critics of the new century. The *Sun* showed them their own country, and gave them eyes to see it clearly. It created among them a sophisticated and highly civilized point of view. It rid them of the national fear of ideas, the national dread of being natural.

How Dana accomplished all this remains a bit dim, even in Mr. Mitchell's chronicle. There was apparently no formal instruction in the *Sun* office, and certainly none of the harsh discipline which makes the modern city-room like a school-room or a bank. Dana did his own work casually and easily, and seems to have let his men run on in the same way. He was extremely tolerant of drunkards, as he was, in his reception-room, of cranks. He gathered recruits wherever he could, and without too much care. But the massive fact remains that, once he had gathered them, he converted them quickly into journalists of a new, unmatched and superior kind. The commonest treadmill work on his paper was done in a lively and excellent manner; its very sporting news, on most papers frankly idiotic, was distinguished. All of his men wrote good English; all of them had sharp eyes; all of them gathered something of his shrewd wisdom. Many of them, graduating from his staff, went in for literature in the grand manner, and did work of importance: I need point only to David Graham Phillips as an example—a man of immense influence upon the course of the American novel. But more important still were the men who were taught their trade by the *Sun* without ever having worked for it. Think of all those who were influenced by the criticism of James Huneker, a thorough *Sun* man to the end of his days, never happy on any other paper! I have elsewhere discussed him at length; when the record is written at last, if it is ever written honestly, he will stand among the genuine makers of American literature, though his own books be forgotten. What Huneker had to teach was precisely what the *Sun* in general had to teach: the stupidity of pedantry and all formal knowledge, the charm and virtue of fresh observation and hearty joy in life.

Mr. Mitchell's book covers an almost incredible space; he served a round fifty years on the *Sun,* beginning as an occasional correspondent and ending as editor-in-chief. Even for a newspaper editor he managed to keep himself well-hidden; I doubt that one of his readers in a hundred ever heard of him. Within the ranks of journalism itself he was a singularly vague and retiring figure: such men as Ochs, Watterson, Reick and Ogden were much more talked of. When he retired at last there was a public dinner for him—by a grotesque turn of fate, one of the very clown-shows, so solemn and so deadly, that the *Sun* itself used to fall upon with such delight.

"At the dais table figured the proprietors . . . of the *Herald*, the *Tribune*, . . . the Brooklyn *Eagle*." Telegrams were received from the Hon. Mr. Harding, the Hon. Mr. Coolidge, the Hon. Will H. Hays, the Hon. James M. Beck. But that was not enough. The obscenity had to be piled on: the three formal speeches were made by two politicians and the Hon. Frank A. Munsey! . . . Mr. Mitchell is still alive and in excellent health. I propose that he be invited to another dinner, and that the subscribers be old readers of the *Sun*. They are scattered over the country, in some places very thinly. I believe that they constitute what I have hitherto denominated, to the scandal of patriots, the civilized minority—that is, the elder part of it. The youngsters who have grown up since 1916 have no memory of the *Sun* to cheer them. . . .

10

A Wholesaler in Journalism

(A review of *Forty Years in Newspaperdom,* by Milton A. McRae.
The American Mercury, January 1925.)

This McRae, now retired, was for years the field manager and
general handy man of the Scripps-McRae league of newspapers,
founded by his partner, Edward W. Scripps. Scripps still survives
at seventy, a hearty old buck, still smoking forty cigars a day and
still full of enterprise and even pugnacity. He is probably the most
successful newspaper owner America has ever known, and yet he
is seldom heard of. Hearst and Munsey get a hundred times as
much notice; even old Cyrus H. K. Curtis and young Ned McLean
are far better known. Yet Scripps has probably made more money
out of daily newspapers than all of them lumped together, and his
papers are in a sounder position than theirs today. Perhaps his
obscurity is due to the fact that most of his sheets are published in
small towns, and that those that are not still bear a small-town air.
The best of them is the Cleveland *Press,* an immensely valuable
property and so influential that it carried Cleveland for La Follette
at the last election. Yet when newspaper men think of Cleveland
they usually think of the *Plain Dealer,* a paper of much less
importance. The *Plain Dealer,* indeed, is a poor stick, even as
newspapers go in the provinces, but it at least maintains a sort of

94

metropolitan air, and aims to lead the Best Thought of its town. The Scripps papers are all aimed frankly at the common people.

Scripps himself has never written a book, and it is extremely doubtful that he ever will. He is not the kind of man who delights in self-exposure; he is far too intelligent (and maybe I should add too cynical) to posture as a great leader of thought. McRae is a much more naïve fellow. His autobiography, in fact, is a dreadful give-away of him, and of the civilization which enabled him to amass millions moulding public opinion. His own opinion, it appears, is substantially that of any respectable owner of a door-knob factory, a prosperous lime and cement business, or a chain of one-arm lunch-rooms. He is, as he depicts himself, Babbitt to the life. It is his delight in his retirement—he was rich at forty-nine—to tour the country addressing "Y.M.C.A.'s, colleges, Chambers of Commerce, realty boards, Boy Scouts' meetings, and other organizations." The perfect Rotarian. The ideal of Kiwanis. He has served as director-general of many drives. The Boy Scouts owe much to him. He believes that the Y.M.C.A. is a great moral force. His book is adorned with letters from Presidents of the United States, some of them in proud facsimile, certifying that he is "a gentleman of wide experience in public affairs, and of the highest business and social standing," and calling upon all diplomatic and consular officers of the United States to be polite to him. Curiously enough, the letter of the martyred McKinley, dated August 3, 1896, and that of the illustrious Roosevelt, dated April 20, 1907, are in almost precisely the same words. Can it be that a form is kept for such documents? Or did McRae dictate the text himself?

The Scripps papers do not run to literary finish, and so it is not surprising to find one of their owners writing very badly. What *is* surprising is to find such a man as he depicts owning papers that are so advanced, and even radical, in their politics. How does he square his eloquence before Chambers of Commerce and realty boards with their support of the Bolshevik monster, La Follette? Perhaps the answer is to be found in the fact that he is no longer engaged actively in their management. But a good deal of his money, I take it, is still in them, and so I fancy that they must sometimes give him disquiet. Certainly not, however, as properties, for there are no more profitable papers in the United States. What is more, the profits are not all hogged by the owners. In every

Scripps-McRae (or, as they are now called, Scripps-Howard) paper, the chief men in both editorial and business offices have shares, and in some cases those shares are very valuable. Who invented this system, whether Scripps or McRae, I don't know, but it has certainly worked very well. The slaves work like Trojans in order to deliver themselves from slavery, and many of them succeed. All over this great free land there are ex-reporters and former advertisement solicitors rolling around in Packards and smoking thirty-cent cigars. They are the alumni of Scripps-McRae papers. The Munsey papers, I believe, turn out very few such graduates.

11

Joseph Pulitzer

(A review of *Joseph Pulitzer: His Life and Letters,* by Don C. Seitz. *The American Mercury,* February 1925)

Mr. Seitz served on the *World* under Mr. Pulitzer for sixteen years and is still a high officer of the paper, with the rank of *Generaloberst* at least. His view of his old chief is thus extremely friendly and even partial, but it would be unjust to speak of his book as mere special pleading. On the contrary, it is full of evidence that he had made up his mind, when he sat down to write it, to tell the truth —that he was resolved to depict, not a pewter hero, shining with transcendental light, but the veritable man. That resolve is carried out with very few reservations. We not only see Pulitzer when he was brilliant, which was surely not every day; we also see him when he was foolish, which was probably much oftener. We are made privy to his singular and multitudinous vanities, to his curious hypocrisies and inconsistencies, to his swift descents from the boldness of a lion to the caution of a cat, to his peculiar talent for tyranny and injustice. The man suffered a good deal from adulation during his life-time, and there has been a tendency to gild him absurdly since his death. Mr. Seitz knocks off much of the gilt, and so restores the authentic Pulitzer, his head in the clouds but his feet always rooted firmly in the clay of earth. He becomes comprehensible; more, he becomes charming. One puts down the book with the feeling that, whatever his weaknesses and mountebankeries, he remained at bottom a genuinely interesting man—that his proverbial luck was mainly made by himself—that there was a brain in his head that differed greatly from the common brains of humankind, and that he had trained it to work with efficiency. He had more ideas in a day than most men have in a year. And he left a deeper mark upon his time than most men with ten times his opportunities.

Seitz disposes of large sections of the Pulitzer legend at the very start, and in a few pages. There is, for example, the fable that Pulitzer came to America as a waiter and practiced that profession for years. Park Row, a few years back, was full of journalistic derelicts who alleged that he had once waited on them; some of them added that their tips had enabled him to buy the *World*. The fact is that his service with towel and apron lasted but a part of one day, and that his total tips probably did not run to twenty cents. Nor was he the abject steerage fowl that gossip has made him. His father was a prosperous grain dealer in Hungary, and had made enough money, when young Joseph was a boy of six, to retire to Budapest. His mother, a lady of excellent family, had two brothers who were officers in the Austrian army. It was the death of his father and his mother's remarriage that set the youngster to wandering. First he tried for an Austrian commission, but was rejected because of his weak eyes and frail frame. Then he tried to join the French Foreign Legion in Paris, and failed for the same reason. Then he went to London, and failed yet again. Then to Hamburg, where he sought a berth as a sailor. Rejected a fourth time, he found a friend in a 100% American who shipped him to the United States to join the Union Army, for the Civil War was then raging. He served six months or so in the First New York Cavalry, never seeing any very exciting service, and then came Appomattox, and he was out of a job. His company had been made up chiefly of Germans; he wanted to go somewhere where he could learn English. A practical joker sent him to St. Louis. There, after a few struggles, he quickly made his way. In a few years he was editor of a German newspaper. A few years more, and he was a member of the Missouri Legislature. A few more, and the rudiments of the *Post-Dispatch* were in his hands, and his march to fortune was begun. By the time he was thirty he was a man of means and leisure. When he married, in 1878, fourteen years after his arrival in America, he took his bride to Europe. He had meanwhile got himself admitted to the District of Columbia bar, and vacillated for a time between practicing law and going in for politics. He was already a favorite spellbinder, especially among the German voters, and once actually challenged the mighty Carl Schurz to a debate.

How he happened to buy the *World*—a sort of accident—is an old story; Mr. Seitz adds many details, but they are unimportant. The real drama of his life began after he had run up his flag in Park Row. What he accomplished during the next ten years was a technical feat of immense magnitude and almost inconceivable difficulty—the most complex and arduous ever attempted, perhaps, in the entire history of journalism. On the one hand he set himself the task of creating a newspaper that should be vastly more popular than any paper had ever been before, and on the other hand he essayed to reform and reorganize the whole theory of political journalism—to set up a journal that should be in politics up to the hips, day in and day out, and yet should steer absolutely clear of all party entanglements. The second enterprise was more difficult, I believe, than the first, for it went counter to every idea that then prevailed in the craft. The journalistic imagination of the time was too feeble, indeed, to grasp Pulitzer's notion. It could imagine a trivial, trashy and irresponsible paper, such as Bennett's *Herald,* or a faithful party hack, such as Whitelaw Reid's *Tribune,* or a purely personal organ, such as Dana's *Sun,* but it could not imagine a paper that should be in politics, actively and even passionately, and yet retain complete independence. Pulitzer was a Democrat—in fact, he had swallowed the Jefferson gospel almost in toto—but his chief onslaughts, once he got his legs, were upon Democratic idols. His forays against Tammany, of course, were unimportant; even the *Times* had shown the way there. But when he tackled Cleveland, and then Bryan, he attracted national attention, for such things, in those days, were simply not done. But they paid. Pulitzer fetched the mob with colored comics, black headlines, all the depressing machinery of sensationalism, but he also fetched the civilized minority with his editorial page. Upon that page he lavished all his ingenuity, all his boldness, all his peculiar talent for detecting popular causes. The rest of the paper interested him very little; Seitz shows him referring to it only to damn it as vulgar, idiotic and disgraceful; his own contributions were always to the editorial page. The tumultuous flow of ideas that he turned into it made it, in the end, of country-wide influence, and when the *Sun* began to decline it took an undisputed first place. That place it holds to this day.

But only, I believe, by reason of the fact that no second Pulitzer has yet appeared in New York—or, indeed, anywhere in the country—to challenge it and make the next inevitable step. Pulitzer himself, had he lived, would have made it. That step, obviously enough, lies in the direction of complete emancipation from the current political system—a complete throwing overboard of all the central democratic delusions. The *World,* in the last campaign, supported Davis, the Wall Street lawyer; its chief disciple, the Baltimore *Sun,* followed it. Both papers quickly got into difficulties, for both had to maintain the doctrine that Davis was better than Coolidge—in fact, immensely better. His own speeches proved that this was nonsense, and so his two champions, toward the end of the campaign, puffed and floundered painfully, and went down finally to an embarrassing defeat. In some future national campaign either the one or the other of them—or perhaps some third paper, as yet unsuspected of intelligence—will advance into genuine realism, and so tell the whole truth about *all* of the candidates. Out of that innovation will come the first light that has dawned in our politics since the Jackson *Putsch* of 1828. For it will begin the great work of ridding the American people of the superstition that the way to get better government is to heave one charlatan out and another in—of the abysmal nonsense that there is actually any difference between politicians, that some are devils and the others angels. As I say, I cherish the belief that Pulitzer, had he lived, would have revolted against that nonsense soon or late—that he would have made supporting such a transparent mountebank as Davis punishable by death in the *World* office— death following dreadful tortures. His heirs and assigns imitated the Pulitzer of 1896. They overlooked the fact that the Pulitzer of 1896 was already far ahead of the Pulitzer of 1884, and that he was still making very good speed. Ah, that such men could be reprieved by God, and last a century!

Mr. Seitz's picture of the private and often highly erratic Pulitzer, with his vast staff of secretaries, his laborious and aimless travels, his pathological sensitiveness to noise, his cruel manhandling of his men, his curious streaks of cowardice and his great cunning at getting money—this picture is full of humors. But the extravagances of the comedian never obscure the fact that the workings of a truly brilliant mind were hidden in them—that Pulitzer, at his worst, was still a fellow of gigantic force and originality, and of very real dignity. In all newspaper proprietors, as in all working newspaper men, something of the zany is to be found: it goes with the profession. A man competent to manage so vast and complex an organization as that of a modern newspaper would not devote himself, if he lacked that touch of the gipsy, to such an enterprise: he would go into banking, commerce or something else of complete respectability. Just as every theatrical manager is primarily a gambler, so every journalist is primarily a sort of vagabond. He enjoys adventure and turmoil. He'd rather be where the stinkbombs are going off and innocent thousands are losing their arms and legs than sit all day in a steel bank, protected even from drive managers and rats. He has the romantic and experimental mind. When, as sometimes happens, age brings him wisdom, he retires from journalism. Even Munsey and Curtis, though they appear to be fish, have this puckish quality concealed in them. They are, among fish, somewhat rash and reckless—salmon with vine-leaves in their hair. Pulitzer was a gorgeous porpoise with red, blue and purple spots, streaking through phosphorescent seas, forever lashing his tail.

12

Reflections on Journalism

(Chicago *Tribune*, April 19, 1925)

When I was a young reporter, in the declining years of the last century, the only existing textbook of journalism that had any practical value was the *Steps Into Journalism* of Edwin L. Shuman, then literary editor of the Chicago *Tribune*. The more ancient journalists of the time disdained it, as they did, indeed, all other books. But we younger fellows gave it hard study, and took to heart its doctrine, and presently the sniffish ancients were working for us.

Today the ambitious novice has a whole shelf of books to aid him—nay, almost a library. There are at least a dozen general textbooks as good as Shuman's, and four or five that are vastly better. In addition, there are scores of treatises on definite branches of the craft: editorial writing, copy reading, making up, the work of the city editor, and so on; and useful handbooks of such auxiliary sciences as photo engraving and the law of libel. Many such books, of course, are hack jobs, done by blowsy pedagogues. But among them are also some extremely competent volumes by first rate newspaper men, and the youngster who gives a diligent year to them will emerge with far more sound and useful professional knowledge than his predecessor of the last generation could get out of five years in a city room.

The old time city room, in truth, was a poor school, and I say so with melancholy who graduated from it and still look back upon it with great affection. It was full of pleasant fellows, but the majority of them were bad journalists, for what they mistook for professional knowledge was simply a huge accumulation of useless facts. They had the minds of railway mail clerks. To the fundamental problems of their craft they apparently gave no thought; or, if they did, it was furtively and diffidently. Such grave questions were for editorial writers, managing editors, business managers, owners, and other such superior fauna. Thus there was little professional spirit in the city room, despite its exalted esprit de corps. The boys were not like fellow doctors or fellow lawyers; they were more like fellow Elks.

I believe that the new schools of journalism have changed all that. Many of them, to be sure, are still in a primitive stage, and some are still staffed by obvious incompetents, but in the best of them there are very good teachers, and these teachers are turning out graduates with a lively sense of the essential dignity of journalism, and a determination to safeguard it, as far as possible, in their practice of it. For a while, perhaps, they will have hard sledding, for old timers still reign in most American newspaper offices, and of all hunkers there is none more hunkerous than the ancient journalist. But soon or later the youngsters will get on top. When they do so there will be an immense improvement in American journalism.

Already, indeed, the signs of it are visible. It runs in two directions. First, the individual reporter tends to be a more dignified fellow than he once was. Better educated and more competent in his days of beginning, he is far more careful of his amour propre than he used to be. He reads more and drinks less. He demands, and gets, more salary. He is less easily snared by the temptations set for him. His view of his craft takes on a breadth that it never had in the old days. Gradually he ceases to think of it as a game, and begins to think of it as a profession. In actuality, of course, it is not yet a profession, for its practitioners yet lack professional autonomy and authority and the power to enforce discipline within their own ranks—but I believe it is on its way.

This improvement in the individual journalist has had the inevitable effect of improving newspapers. They are no longer as cheap and venal as they used to be. The old timers conveniently forget how bad most of the papers they once worked for really were. In the town where I began there were five sheets, and three of them played dubious politics and leaped whenever an advertiser blew his nose. Every American city was full of such papers; not a few of them made great pretensions. Today, I believe they are rare. The consolidations that every ancient journalist deplores have accomplished at least one good thing: they have got newspapers out of the hands of needy men. And if such men came back tomorrow they would have a hard time inducing competent newspaper men to work for them. The trade has gone up a peg, and it will stay there.

It would move faster if newspaper editors, as a class, were as intelligent as newspaper reporters. I believe that, in the average American town, they are not—that their greater average age puts them back, professionally, almost a generation. The schools of journalism far surpass the old time city rooms in the character of the recruits they enlist. They tap a supply of candidates of better education, and out of much better surroundings. They do not try to make journalists out of busted lawyers, former whisky drummers, and unfrocked clergymen. But many a city desk is still occupied by a city editor of the ice wagon driver school. So long as such silurians survive the value of the work being done by the schools of journalism will not be fully apparent, for that work will not be fully utilized.

Already, however, the more intelligent newspaper editors are utilizing it, and before long, I believe, there will be an active interplay of effort between the schools and newspapers. The schools themselves are trying to raise and safeguard their own standards; the good ones gradually separate themselves from the bad ones, and adopt programs that give them professional dignity. Soon or late the Class A schools, demanding sound educational qualifications for entrance and offering well planned and thorough courses of study, will be sharply differentiated from the one room schools that now flourish, just as the Class A medical and law schools are differentiated from the other kind. When that time comes the graduate of a Class A school will be practically assured of a good job on a good paper the day he graduates.

Everything beyond that will be in the hands not of the pedagogues but of newspaper editors. Once they begin to refuse to employ novices not properly trained, and in Class A schools, journalism will begin to take on professional dignity at last. I speak of the editors of first rate newspapers. Plenty of jobs on the other kind will remain for incompetents. But there will then be just as much difference between a first rate journalist on a first rate paper and the hireling of a gutter sheet as there now is between a graduate of the Harvard medical school and a traveling corn doctor.

As I have said, many of the old timers deplore and oppose the change. Their opposition is not entirely stupid. They get an appearance of logic into it; they believe true journalists can be made in only one way, and that is by throwing them overboard, in youth, in large batches, and watching the fittest survive. There is some plausibility here. In certain of its branches, at all events, success in journalism seems to depend upon a natural bent far more than upon training. I have known men to become very good reporters in three months—as good, in many ways, as the best. But not many. The overwhelming majority have to be taught—and if they are ever to escape from the ranks they have to be taught some more. I believe that most of this teaching can be done more conveniently in school than in a city room—that the novice who has been competently trained will be much more useful and make much faster progress than the poor fellow who has to comb a city editor's profanity for its occasional strands of wisdom.

The stray genius need not be taken into account. No newspaper, I greatly fear, was ever manned by geniuses alone; Richard Harding Davis would probably have made a bad night editor or editorial writer. Most of the hard work must be done by men who depend less upon inspiration than upon sound professional competence. The greater the competence of such men, the more accurate, intelligent, and useful are our newspapers. And the greater their sense of professional dignity, the more honorable and conscientious is the craft they practice. I believe schools of journalism tend to improve them in both directions.

Mencken at the beginning and end of his long newspaper career. Above is the 21-year-old star of the Baltimore *Herald*. Below, Mencken on his 70th birthday leans to blow out candles at a party in the board room of the *Sunpapers*. *Sun* political columnist Frank R. Kent sits on his right; *Sunpapers* President William Schmick, Sr., on his left.

Baltimore newspaper readers were curious about the outrageous Free Lance columnist in the *Evening Sun*. So when Mencken began a Sunday article as well, *Sunday Sun* artist McKee Barclay provided the portrait to the left, identified as a photo by Bachrach. Below is the real Free Lance by Bachrach that year, which was 1913.

Mencken is shown above in the study at his home, where most of his Monday Articles were written. The photo was made in 1928. Below is Mencken pecking away frenziedly to meet a deadline while covering a national party convention in 1932.

Mencken as editor of the *Evening Sun* in 1938. He was technically acting editor, but despite that, and despite the posed appearance of the above photo, it was a real job that he threw himself into with gusto. In the bottom picture Mencken is shown writing one of his last newspaper dispatches, from the 1948 Progressive Party convention in Philadelphia.

13

Learning How to Blush

(A review of *The Conscience of the Newspaper*, by Leon Nelson Flint.
The American Mercury, July 1925)

This fat and solemn book, by the professor of journalism at the University of Kansas, is typical of the soul-searching that now seems to be going on in American journalism. When I was a young reporter, a quarter of a century ago, nothing of the sort was visible. The journalists of those days—or, at all events, those under the age of sixty—were unanimously convinced that they practiced a noble art, or, as they affected to call it, business, and that its public uses were lofty and indubitable. Here and there, to be sure, one found a purist who had something to say against the new yellowness, endemic since the Spanish-American War, and somewhat more often one heard murmurs against the low pay of journalists and the tyrannical ways of business managers. But such complaints were surely not numerous, nor was there any general discontent under them. The normal, right-thinking reporter of the time believed that journalism was fundamentally healthy and virtuous, and that every day in every way it was growing better and better. One questioning its essential worth and dignity would have amazed him as genuinely as one questioning democracy, baseball or the saloon business. He simply had no room in his head for doubts.

But now his head seems to buzz with them. Every time a disabled journalist is retired to a professorship in a school of journalism, and so gets time to give sober thought to the state of his craft, he seems to be impelled to write a book upon its ethics, full of sour and uraemic stuff. How many such volumes have come out of late I don't know, but there must be dozens of them. Worse, the state editorial associations and other such sanhedrins of journalists fling themselves upon the same melancholy subject, and so it gets a constant and malodorous ventilation. I have read, during the past year, at least twenty proposed codes of journalistic ethics, many of them so heavy with dark innuendo that going through them has made me sad indeed. No two of them are alike; they run the whole scale from metaphysical principalia worthy of Rotary to sets of rules fit for the government of a *Zuchthaus*. But in all of them there is the plain implication that journalism is bespattered with boils, and that they stand in need of prompt and radical surgery.

As I have hitherto hinted in this place, I have no great confidence in these new codes of ethics. Most of them are the work of journalists of no professional importance, and, what is worse, of very little apparent sense. They concern themselves furiously with abuses which are not peculiar to journalism but run through the whole of American life, and they are delicately silent about abuses that are wholly journalistic, and could be remedied quickly and without the slightest difficulty. Their purpose, I believe, is largely rhetorical. They give a certain ease and comfort without letting any of the patient's blood. Nevertheless, I am glad to see them multiply, for though most of them may be hollow today, there is always a chance that some solid substance may get into them tomorrow. If they accomplish nothing else at the moment, they at least accustom the journalist to the notion that his craft needs improvement. His old romantic optimism oozes out of him. He is no longer quite happy. Out of his rising discomforts, I believe, there will issue eventually a more realistic attitude toward the problems that confront him, and on some bright day in the future he may address himself rationally to the hard business of solving them. Most of them are clearly soluble. More, most of them can be solved by working newspaper men, without any help from experts in ethics. What they call for is not any transcendental gift for righteousness, but simply common sense.

For example, the problem of false news, which Prof. Flint, following most of his predecessors, discusses at great length—that is, the problem of ascertaining and printing the truth, or, at all events, the nearest attainable approximation to it. How does so much of this false news get into the newspapers? Is it because journalists, as a class, are habitual liars, and prefer what is not true to what is true? I don't think it is. Rather, it is because journalists are, in the main, extremely sentimental and credulous fellows—because nothing is easier than to fool them—because the majority of them lack the sharp intelligence that the proper discharge of their duties demands. The New York *Times* did not print its famous blather and balderdash about Russia because the Hon. Mr. Ochs desired to deceive his customers, or because his slaves were in the pay of Russian reactionaries, but simply and solely because those slaves, facing the elemental professional problems of distinguishing between true news and false, proved themselves incompetent. All around the borders of Russia sat propagandists hired to fool them. In many cases, I have no doubt, they detected that purpose, and foiled it; we only know what they printed, not what they threw into their waste-baskets. But in many other cases they succumbed easily, and even humorously, and the result was the vast mass of puerile rubbish that Mr. Lippmann later made a show of. In other words, the editors of the American newspaper most brilliantly distinguished above its fellows for its news-gathering turned out to be unequal to a job of news-gathering presenting special difficulties. It was not an ethical failure, but a purely technical failure.

Obviously, the way to diminish such failures in the future is not to adopt codes of sonorous platitudes borrowed from the realtors, the morticians, the sanitary plumbers and Kiwanis, but to undertake an overhauling of the faulty technic, and of the incompetent personnel responsible for it. This overhauling, of course, will take some intelligence, but I don't think it will make demands that are impossible. The bootlegging, legal or delicatessen professions, confronted by like demands, would quickly furnish the talent necessary to meet them; I see no reason why the profession of journalism should not measure up as well. What lies in the way of it is simply the profound and maudlin credulity of the average American journalist—his ingenuous and almost automatic belief in everything that comes to him in writing. One would think that his daily experience with the written word would make him suspicious of it; he himself, in fact, believes fondly that he is proof against it. But the truth is that he swallows it far more often than he rejects it, and that his most eager swallowing is done in the face of the plainest evidence of its falsity. Let it come in by telegraph, and his mouth flies open. Let it come in by telegraph *from a press association,* and down it goes at once. I do not say, of course, that *all* press association news is thus swallowed by news editors. When the means are readily at hand, he often attempts to check it, and sometimes even rejects it. But when such checking presents difficulties—in other words, when deceit is especially easy, and hence should be guarded against most vigilantly—he succumbs nine times out of ten, and without a struggle. It was precisely by this process that the editors of the *Times,* otherwise men of extraordinary professional alertness, were victimized by the Russian "news" that made their paper ridiculous. In the face of great improbabilities, they interpreted their inability to dispose of them as a license to accept them as truth. Journalism will be a sounder and more dignified profession when a directly contrary interpretation of the journalist's duty prevails. There will then be less news in the papers, but it will at least have the merit of being true.

Nor is the journalist's credulity confined to such canards and roorbacks from far places. He is often victimized just as easily at home, despite his lofty belief that he is superior to the wiles of press agents. The plain fact is that most of the stuff he prints now emanates from press agents, and that his machinery for scrutinizing it is lamentably defective. True enough, the bold, gay liars employed by theatrical managers and opera singers no longer fool him as they used to; he has grown so suspicious of them that he often turns them out when they have real news. But what of the press agents of such organizations as the Red Cross, the Prohibition Unit, the Near-East Relief, the Chamber of Commerce of the United States, the Department of Justice, the Y.M.C.A., and the various bands of professional patriots? I do not say that the press agents of such bodies are always or necessarily liars; all I say is that, nine times out of ten, their statements are accepted as true by the newspapers without any attempt to determine accurately whether they are true or not. They may be simple statements of plain fact; they may, on the contrary, conceal highly dubious purposes, of organizations or individuals. In both cases they are set forth in the same way—solemnly and without comment. Who, ordinarily, would believe a Prohibition agent? Perhaps a Federal judge in his robes of office; I can think of no one else. Yet the newspapers are filled every day with the dreadful boasts and threats of such frauds; they are set before the people, not as lies, but as news. What is the purpose of such bilge? Its purpose, obviously, is to make it appear that the authors are actually enforcing Prohibition—in other words, to make them secure in their jobs. Every newspaper man in America knows that Prohibition is not being enforced—and yet it is rarely that an American newspaper comes out in these days without a gaudy story on its first page, rehearsing all the old lies under new and blacker headlines.

I do not argue here, of course, that only demonstrable facts are news. There are times and occasions when rumor is almost as important as the truth—when a newspaper's duty to its readers requires it to tell them not only what has happened, but also what is reported, what is threatened, what is merely said. What I contend is simply that such quasi-news, such half-baked and still dubious news, should be printed for exactly what it is—that it ought to be clearly differentiated from news that, by an overwhelming probability, is true. That differentiation is made easily and as a matter of course by most European newspapers of any dignity. When they print a dispatch from the Russian border they indicate its source, and not infrequently follow it with a cynical comment. If they had Prohibition agents on their hands, they would print the fulminations of those gentlemen in the same way—with plain warnings to stop, look and listen. In brief, they make every reasonable effort to make up for their own technical limitations as news-gatherers— they do the best they can, and say so frankly when it is not very good. I believe that American newspapers might imitate them profitably. If it were done, then the public's justifiable distrust of all newspapers, now rising steadily, would tend to ebb. They would have to throw off their present affectation of omniscience, but they would gain a new name for honesty and candor; they would begin to seem more reliable when they failed than they now seem when they succeed. The scheme I propose would cost nothing; on the contrary, it would probably save expense. It would throw no unbearable burden upon the journalistic mind; it would simply make it more cautious and alert. Best of it, it would increase the dignity of journalism without recourse to flapdoodlish and unenforceable codes of ethics, by Mush out of Tosh. As I have said, those clodes seem to me to miss every mark they are aimed at. They seek to convert the journalist into a Good Man, an Idealist; he is in point of fact, nothing of the sort, but a fellow who likes to look at the human show from a stage box, and to laugh at it. I dedicate my plan respectfully to the profession I have so long adorned.

14

More Tips for Novelists

(Chicago *Tribune*, May 2, 1926)

. . . Even some of the most salient and arresting of American types lack historians and seem doomed to perish and be forgotten with the Bill of Rights. Babbitt stood around for a dozen years waiting for Lewis; the rest of the novelists of the land gaped at him without seeing him. How long will they gape at the American politician? At the American university president? At the American policeman? At the American lawyer? At the American insurance man? At the prohibition fanatic? At the revival evangelist? At the bootlegger? At the Y.M.C.A. secretary? At the butter and egg man? At the journalist?

Above all, the journalists! Most American novelists, before they challenge Dostoevski, put in an apprenticeship on the public prints, and so they have a chance to study and grasp the peculiarities of the journalistic mind; nevertheless, the fact remains that there is not a single genuine newspaper man, done in the grand manner, in the whole range of American fiction. There are some excellent brief sketches, but there is no adequate portrait of the journalist as a whole, from his beginnings as a romantic young reporter to his finish as a Babbitt, correct in every idea and as hollow as a jug.

Here, I believe, is genuine tragedy. Here is the matter that enters into all fiction of the first class. Here is a human character in disintegration—the primary theme of every sound novelist ever heard of, from Fielding to Zola and from Turgenev to Joseph Conrad. I know of no American who starts from a higher level of aspiration than the journalist. He is, in his first phase, genuinely

116

romantic. He plans to be both an artist and a moralist—a master of lovely words and a merchant of sound ideas. He ends, commonly, as the most depressing jackass in his community—that is, if his career goes on to what is called success. He becomes the repository of all its worst delusions and superstitions. He becomes the darling of all its frauds and idiots and the despair of all its honest men. He belongs to a good club, and the initiation fee was his soul.

Here I speak by the book, for I have been in active practice as a journalist for more than a quarter of a century and have an immense acquaintance in the craft. I could name a man who fits my specifications exactly in every American city east of the Mississippi, and refrain only on the advice of counsel. I do not say that all journalists go that route. Far from it! Many escape by failing; some even escape by succeeding. But the majority succumb. They begin with high hopes. They end with safe jobs.

In the career of any such men, it seems to me, there are materials for fiction of the highest order. He is interesting intrinsically, for his early ambition is at least not ignoble—he is not a born earthworm. And he is interesting as a figure in drama, for he falls gradually, resisting all the while, to forces that are beyond his strength. If he can't make the grade it is not because he is unwilling or weak, but because the grade itself is too steep. Here is tragedy— and here is America. For the curse of this country, as of all democracies, is precisely the fact that it treats its best men as enemies. The aim of our society, if it may be said to have an aim, is to iron them out. The ideal American, in the public sense, is a respectable vacuum.

I heave this typical American journalist to the massed novelists of the Federal Union and invite them to lay on. There is a capital novel in him—a capital character sketch and a capital picture of the American scene. He is representative and yet he is not commonplace. People will recognize him, and yet they are not familiar with him. Let the fictioneers have at him! But let them bear in mind that he is not to be done to the tune of superior sneers. He is a wreck, but he has not succumbed to the gales without resistance. Let him be done ironically, as Lewis did Babbitt, but let him be done also with pity. He is not a comedian, but a tragedian. Above all, let him be done without any mouthing of theories. His simple story is poignant enough.

117

15

Notes on Journalism

(Chicago *Tribune*, September 19, 1926)

The general success of the tabloid papers, the oldest of which is only seven years old, still seems to puzzle the majority of newspaper men. When they admit it at all they commonly credit it to the looseness and imbecility of the newcomers, which are described as given over wholly to crime and scandal. But this is plainly a prejudiced and highly inaccurate view of them. In the whole country there are not more than three actually specialized in such matters. The rest at worst are no worse than the usual run of yellows. And at best they are very good newspapers, intelligently edited and carefully printed.

What makes them popular, I believe, is far less their contents than their form. They are made for reading in crowds, and it is in crowds that they are mainly read. A great advertising boom now rages in the United States, and all the oldline papers run to an immense bulkiness. Some of the more prosperous of them, on the days that advertisers favor, come out in two or three sections and weigh a pound or more. To go through such a paper in a jammed street car is quite impossible. The man who attempts it gets only a beating for his pains. But he can manage a tabloid without making his neighbors yell, and so he reads it.

The lightness of the little papers gives them another advantage; they can be distributed much more quickly than the larger papers. A boy on a motor cycle can carry a hundred copies of even the bulkiest of them to a remote junction in ten or twenty minutes, but the old-style papers have to go by truck, which is slower. Not so many can be printed in an hour. Not so many can be carried by a single newsboy. These advantages count up. The majority of readers, when there is news afloat that interests them seriously, look for it in the larger papers, which can give it in full. But these same readers also buy the tabloids for the first bulletins. Thus there is much duplication of circulation. The tabloids take a certain amount of circulation away from the larger papers, but not enough to be disastrous.

II

They would be even more successful than they are, I believe, if their editors could resist the temptation to improve them. That temptation, of course, is easy to understand. Every newspaper man worthy of the name dreams of making his paper better than it is, and those who run the tabloids are stimulated further by the general professional opinion that their papers are somehow low. So every tabloid, as soon as it gets into safe waters, begins to grow intellectual. The bald, gaudy devices that launched it are abandoned and it takes on decorum. Already there are tabloids with opinions on the French debt, the Philippine question and the music of Stravinsky. I know at least two that are actually liberal.

This, I fear, is a false form of progress. The tabloid, so lifted by its bootstraps, becomes simply a little newspaper, and it must inevitably be inferior to the big ones. If I were a tabloid magnate I'd head in the other direction. That is to say, I'd try to produce a paper interesting and instructive to the uncounted thousands who now read no newspaper at all. That such persons exist may seem incredible, but it is nevertheless a fact. They swarm in every large American city. They include the vast class of illiterates, which is everywhere larger than the statistics show. And they include the even larger class of near-illiterates—that is, those who are able to spell out enough words to get them through the ordinary business of life, but find reading so laborious and painful that they avoid it as much as possible.

Many of them, as the psychologist, Dr. Eleanor Wembridge, has demonstrated, are congenitally incapable of mastering it. They understand only such words as are comprehensible to a child of, say, 10. The rest is simply a fog to them. An ordinary newspaper article, even in a tabloid, is thus mainly unintelligible to them. Half the words in it are beyond them. Even when, by dint of hard sweating, they spell their way through it, the impression it leaves upon them is very vague and unsatisfactory. They may grasp its main proposition, but all its details are lost upon them.

III

It is my belief that a newspaper aimed at such readers would make a great success in any large American city, and especially in Chicago or New York. It should be printed throughout, as First Readers are printed, in words of one syllable. It should avoid every idea that is beyond the understanding of a boy of 10. It should print no news about anything that morons are not interested in. And its illustrations, instead of being mere decorations, should really illustrate, as the pictures in a First Reader illustrate.

I don't think it would be difficult to get together a staff for such a paper. If journalism itself failed to produce the necessary talent, recourse might be had to pedagogy. There are schoolma'ams, male and female, all over this great land who are professionally adept at explaining things to children. They have perfected technical devices that do the trick quickly and effectively, and those devices could be adapted to journalism without the slightest difficulty. Journalists themselves, after a little training, would greatly improve them, for journalists as a class are much more intelligent than pedagogues. In the end there would be a new English (or American) for the submerged, and reading would spread to a vast class that now gets all its news by listening.

To that class, as to children, much of what now passes for news, and is dished up in endlesss columns every morning, is wholly uninteresting. Its members, despite the alarm of bank directors and other such naive fellows, are not Socialists; they are, indeed, quite incapable of comprehending politics save as a combat between two men, A and B. In the strict sense, all ideas are beyond them. They can grasp only events. Are they interested only in crime? I don't think so. What they are interested in is drama. The thing presented to them must take the form of a combat, and it must be a very simple combat, with one side clearly right and the other clearly wrong. They can no more imagine neutrality than they can imagine the fourth dimension. And when they see drama they want to see it moving.

IV

Soon or late some sagacious journalist will set up a paper made to the tastes and limitations of this immense horde of God's children, and his rewards will descend upon him like a deluge. The earliest movie magnates tapped that colossal till with great skill, and so lifted the movies to the third (or is it second?) place among the country's industries. They did not start out with Balzac, Joseph Conrad and Dostoevski; they started out with "The Perils of Pauline" and filmizations of serials out of the *Fireside Companion.*

But once they got rich, they began to develop, in the immemorial human way, a yearning to be respectable, and even intellectual. That is, they began to turn their backs upon their original clients, who had poured all their wealth into their coffers, and to reach out for customers of a higher sophistication. Thus, the 10-cent movie house passed into the shadows and in its place appeared the blazing hell showing pictures at $2—pictures full of artistic and even literary pretension. Fortunately for the movie magnates, this pretension was mainly buncombe. They lacked the skill and culture necessary to make the movies genuinely intelligent, and so they escaped bankruptcy. But, even so, they converted a business whose profits were as certain as those of a bootlegger into a business full of hazards and calamities.

They will come to a safe harbor again when they return to the *Fireside Companion* level. No one in this world, so far as I know— and I have searched the records for years, and employed agents to help me—has ever lost money by underestimating the intelligence of the great masses of the plain people. Nor has anyone ever lost public office thereby. The mistake that is made always runs the other way. Because the plain people are able to speak and understand, and even, in many cases, to read and write, it is assumed that they have ideas in their heads, and an appetite for more. This assumption is a folly. They dislike ideas, for ideas make them uncomfortable. The tabloids, seeking to force such things upon them, will inevitably alarm them and lose their trade. The journalism of the future—that is, the mob journalism—will move in the direction that I have indicated.

16

Adams as an Editor

(Baltimore *Evening Sun*, October 14, 1927)

I

Of all the journalists I have known in this life, the late John Haslup Adams, who died yesterday, was the only man who never made a visible compromise with his convictions. Such compromises are very common in the profession, as they are in the law, not to mention medicine and the sacred desk. For journalism is not only a profession; it is also, like the rest, a business—and in business what would be theoretically sweet and nice must always be diluted with what will pay its way. But Adams never seemed to take that fact into his calculations. He had all the virtues of the Puritan— and, at their best, what virtues they are! He could imagine getting beaten for an idea, and even getting beaten by it, but he was quite unable to imagine running away from it.

Basically, he was an old-fashioned Liberal, and of the true Godkin line. The thing he esteemed most in this world was simply fair play. That fact explained most of his politics, which, from the partisan point of view, were often beautifully vague. His hero for a long time was Senator Borah, but I doubt that he subscribed to more than a half of Borah's notions. What attracted him to the man was their common passion for justice. Moreover, Borah himself needed help: all the forces of reaction were trying to pull him down. This aroused Adams, a mild man, to fury. Right or wrong, Borah was honest, and must be heard. Up, guards, and at 'em!

But I think he liked them to be smaller; it was more fun going to the rescue. An injustice to Great Britain did not greatly excite him, but the slightest impoliteness to Nicaragua or Honduras set him off. In his last days he raised a dreadful uproar in *The Sun* office about an obscure subscriber who came in to complain that the police were persecuting him. He gave hours to the man, and ordered an inquiry that cost time and money. If President Willard, of the B.&O., had come in with the same complaint I suspect that he would have had a shorter hearing, for Mr. Willard can afford to hire lawyers. But a poor man facing the cops needed help, and he got it instantly.

II

The Liberals of Adams' early years had a great faith in laws, and he shared that faith until he was well into middle life. There was a time when he had great hopes of such things as the recall, and the initiative and referendum. There was even a time when he had some confidence in Prohibition—a consequence, I dare say, of his Puritan heritage quite as much as of his Liberal politics. Even to the end he believed that Prohibition would be a good thing for the human race—if it could be enforced.

It was the complete failure of the attempt to enforce it that moved him, along with the other Liberals, from old-fashioned Liberalism into libertarianism. In this hegira he had plenty of company—Villard of the *Nation,* Lippmann of the New York *World*—men he respected, and who respected him. These men have all come to a certain distrust of democracy, or, at all events, of the democratic process. But they continue to believe that justice is still possible in the world, if those who favor it will only fight for it hard enough, and in this belief Adams joined them. He went further, indeed, than they did; he never had any doubt of it.

The fact was the cornerstone of his journalistic theory. He saw a great modern newspaper as largely, if not mainly, an engine for rectifying injustice. If it simply printed the news that came in, from anywhere and everywhere, it failed in a prime duty. That duty, he believed, obliged it to go behind the news, to find out whence the news had come and by whom it had been set afloat, to detect and expose any falsity that was in it, or any self-interest. To this business he addressed his chief energies all his life. He was the most indefatigable of men. No point of view, however grotesque, was too grotesque for him to hear it. He believed profoundly that new truths, while they were still new, often sounded like nonsense, and that what made them sound like nonsense was not infrequently only the unfairness of their opponents.

III

His journalistic practice both gained and suffered by this belief. It tended to make him, at times, very cautious, not of consequences, but of ideas themselves. The typical journalist runs to shorter cuts: he is so battered all his days by propaganda that he falls inevitably into a certain cynicism, even when it comes to his own faiths. His decisions must be made quickly, and he naturally likes to make them in the easiest way. But not Adams. He was forever investigating, weighing probabilities, debating with himself. He was always searching for another side, and trying to understand it. It made an admirable fly-wheel of him. He prevented many a lovely editorial wreck. And when the uproar was over, it usually turned out that what he advocated was what everyone saw was the right thing to do.

But about the fundamentals he never had any doubt. The first duty of a newspaper was to find out the facts—not the superficial facts, but the underlying ones, the basic ones. Its second duty was to expound the lesson of those facts—temperately, carefully, but with unbreakable resolution. If doing these things involved a risk, then the risk would have to be taken. He not only believed that this policy was the only one that, in the long run, would make a paper powerful and great; he believed that it was the only one tolerable to a self-respecting journalist. It was better to be wrong a thousand times than to compromise once. But it was never necessary to be wrong. The facts, he believed, would always yield to industry. And between right and wrong there was still a clear line.

As I have said, he had all the virtues of the Puritan. He could never dismiss cruelty and injustice lightly, in the easy way of his craft. He believed that such things were evil, and that what was evil should be put down. But there was absolutely nothing of the wowser about him. He knew too much about professional reformers to be deceived by their pretensions. Their harassing of the helpless did not interest him.

IV

I knew Adams for twenty-seven years, and during many of them we were in daily contact. In 1910 he and I wrote the first editorial page of *The Evening Sun,* and thereafter, for a number of years, I was his chief of staff. That intimacy gave me a very high respect for his professional skill. He was an editorial writer of immense competence, for his mind was packed with facts, and he knew how to write quickly and clearly. Many a time I have seen him, in half an hour, turn out an editorial that was a model of sound information and solid argument. His style was singularly lucid. What he had to say he said simply, and usually briefly. There was no rhetoric in him, but when he thundered it was a dreadful clap indeed.

His later years were oppressed by an illness that was at times almost unbearable. He suffered excruciating pain and for months running would be unable to walk. But always he would bob up again, hobbling into *The Sun* office to see what was afoot. For long periods he did his work in bed. Then he would come back again, full of ideas and eager to get them on paper. His hand was in every major policy of *The Sun* for seventeen years, his influence upon the paper, it seems to me, was incalculably valuable. There was not only the wisdom of his concrete projects; there was also the high example of his gallant character and his indomitable courage. No more honest man ever set pen to paper, and no braver man.

17

Journalism in America

(*Prejudices: Sixth Series*, 1927)

One of the agreeable spiritual phenomena of the great age in which we live is the soul-searching now going on among American journalists. Fifteen years ago, or even ten years ago, there was scarcely a sign of it. The working newspaper men of the Republic, of whom I have had the honor to be one since the last century, were then almost as complacent as so many Federal judges, movie magnates, or major-generals in the army. When they discussed their puissant craft at all, it was only to smack their chests proudly, boasting of their vast power in public matters, of their adamantine resistance to all the less tempting varieties of bribes, and of the fact that a politician of enlightened self-interest, giving them important but inaccurate news confidently, could rely upon them to mangle it beyond recognition before publishing it. I describe a sort of Golden Age, and confess frankly that I can't do so without a certain yielding to emotion. Salaries had been going up since the dawn of the new century, and the journalist, however humble, was beginning to feel his oats. For the first time in history he was paid as well as the human cranes and steam-shovels slinging rolls of paper in the cellar. He began to own two hats, two suits of clothes, two pairs of shoes, two walking-sticks, even two belts. He ceased to feed horribly in one-arm lunch-rooms and began to dine in places with fumigated waitresses, some of a considerable pulchritude and amiability, and red-shaded table lamps. He was, as such things are reckoned, happy. But at the heart of his happiness, alas, there yet gnawed a canker-worm. One enemy remained in his world, unscotched and apparently unscotchable, to wit, the business manager. The business manager, at will, could send up a blue slip and order him fired. In the face of that menace from below-stairs his literary superiors were helpless, up to and including the editor-in-chief. All of them were under the hoof of the business manager, and all the business manager ever thought of was advertising. Let an advertiser complain that his honor had been impugned or his *clavi* abraded, and off went a head.

It was the great war for human freedom, I suspect and allege, that brought the journalist deliverance from that last and most abominable hazard: he was, perhaps, one of the few real beneficiaries of all the carnage. As the struggle grew more savage on Flanders fields and business grew better and better at home, reporters of any capacity whatever got to be far too scarce to fire loosely. Moreover, the business manager, with copy pouring over his desk almost unsolicited, began to lose his old dread of advertisers, and then even some of his natural respect for them. It was a sellers' market, in journalism as in the pants business. Customers were no longer kissed; the lesser among them actually began to stand in line. The new spirit, so strange and so exhilarating, spread like a benign pestilence, and presently it began to invade even the editorial rooms. In almost every American city, large or small, some flabbergasted advertiser, his money in his hand, sweat pouring from him as if he had seen a ghost, was kicked out with spectacular ceremonies. All the principal papers, suddenly grown rich, began also to grow independent, virtuous, touchy, sniffish. No — — — — could dictate to them, God damn! So the old free reading notices of the Bon Marché and the Palais Royal disappeared, salaries continued to climb, and the liberated journalist, taking huge breaths of thrilling air, began to think of himself as a professional man.

Upon that cogitation he is still engaged, and all the weeklies that print the news of the craft are full of its fruits. He elects representatives and they meet in lugubrious conclave to draw up codes of ethics. He begins to read books dealing with professional questions of other sorts—even books not dealing with professional questions. He changes his old cynical view of schools of journalism, and is lured, now and then, into lecturing in them himself. He no longer thinks of his calling as a business, like the haberdasher's or tallow chandler's, or as a game, like the stockbroker's or faro-dealer's, but as a profession, like the jurisconsult's or gynecologist's. His purpose is to set it on its legs as such—to inject plausible theories into its practise, and rid it of its old casualness and opportunism. He no longer sees it as a craft to be mastered in four days, and abandoned at the first sign of a better job. He begins to talk darkly of the long apprenticeship necessary to master its technic, of the wide information and sagacity needed to adorn it, of the high rewards that it offers—or may offer later on—to the man of true talent and devotion. Once he thought of himself, whenever he thought at all, as what Beethoven called a free artist—a gay adventurer careening down the charming highways of the world, the gutter ahead of him but ecstasy in his heart. Now he thinks of himself as a fellow of weight and responsibility, a beginning publicist and public man, sworn to the service of the born and unborn, heavy with duties to the Republic and to his profession.

In all this, I fear, there is some illusion, as there always is in human thinking. The journalist can no more see himself realistically than a bishop can see himself realistically. He gilds and engauds the picture, unconsciously and irresistibly. For one thing, and a most important one, he is probably somewhat in error about his professional status. He remains, for all his dreams, a hired man—the owner downstairs, or even the business manager, though he doesn't do it very often now, is still free to demand his head—and a hired man is not a professional man. The essence of a professional man is that he is answerable for his professional conduct only to his professional peers. A physician cannot be fired by any one, save when he has voluntarily converted himself into a job-holder; he is secure in his livelihood so long as he keeps his health, and can render service, or what they regard as service, to his patients. A lawyer is in the same boat. So is a dentist. So, even, is a horse-doctor. But a journalist still lingers in the twilight zone, along with the trained nurse, the embalmer, the rev. clergy and the great majority of engineers. He cannot sell his services directly to the consumer, but only to entrepreneurs, and so those entrepreneurs have the power of veto over all his soaring fancies. His codes of ethics are all right so long as they do not menace newspaper profits; the moment they do so the business manager, now quiescent, will begin to growl again. Nor has he the same freedom that the lawyers and the physicians have when it comes to fixing his own compensation; what he faces is not a client but a boss. Above all, he is unable, as yet, to control admission to his craft. It is constantly recruited, on its lowest levels, from men who have little professional training or none at all, and some of these men master its chief mysteries very quickly. Thus even the most competent journalist faces at all times a severe competition, easily expanded at need, and cannot afford to be too saucy. When a managing editor is fired there is always another one waiting to take his place, but there is seldom another place waiting for the managing editor.

All these things plainly diminish the autonomy of the journalist, and hamper his effort to lift his trade to professional rank and dignity. When he talks of codes of ethics, indeed, he only too often falls into mere tall talk, for he cannot enforce the rules he so solemnly draws up—that is, in the face of dissent from above. Nevertheless, his discussion of the subject is still not wholly absurd, for there remain plenty of rules that he *can* enforce, and I incline to think that there are more of them than of the other kind. Most of the evils that continue to beset American journalism today, in truth, are not due to the rascality of owners nor even to the Kiwanian bombast of business managers, but simply and solely to the stupidity, cowardice and Philistinism of working newspaper men. The majority of them, in almost every American city, are still ignoramuses, and proud of it. All the knowledge that they pack into their brains is, in every reasonable cultural sense, useless; it is the sort of knowledge that belongs, not to a professional man, but to a police captain, a railway mail-clerk, or a board-boy in a brokerage house. It is a mass of trivialities and puerilities; to recite it would be to make even a barber beg for mercy. What is missing from it, in brief, is everything worth knowing—everything that enters into the common knowledge of educated men. There are managing editors in the United States, and scores of them, who have never heard of Kant or Johannes Müller and never read the Constitution of the

United States; there are city editors who do not know what a symphony is, or a streptococcus, or the Statute of Frauds; there are reporters by the thousand who could not pass the entrance examination for Harvard or Tuskegee, or even Yale. It is this vast and militant ignorance, this widespread and fathomless prejudice against intelligence, that makes American journalism so pathetically feeble and vulgar, and so generally disreputable. A man with so little intellectual enterprise that, dealing with news daily, he can go through life without taking in any news that is worth knowing—such a man, you may be sure, is lacking in professional dignity quite as much as he is lacking in curiosity. The delicate thing called honor can never be a function of stupidity. If it belongs to those men who are genuinely professional men, it belongs to them because they have lifted themselves to the plane of a true aristocracy, in learning as well as in liberty—because they have deliberately and successfully separated themselves from the great masses of men, to whom learning is an insult and liberty an agony. The journalists, in seeking to acquire that status, put the cart before the horse.

2

The facts that I here set forth are well known to every American newspaper man who rises above the ice-wagon driver level, and in those sad conferences which mark every gathering of the craft they do not go undiscussed. Even the American Society of Newspaper Editors, *i.e.*, of those journalists who have got into golf clubs and become minor Babbitts, has dealt with them at some of its annual pow-wows, albeit very gingerly and with many uneasy glances behind the door. But in general journalism suffers from a lack of alert and competent professional criticism; its slaves, afflicted by a natural inferiority complex, discountenance free speaking as a sort of treason; I have myself been damned as a public enemy for calling attention, ever and anon, to the intolerable incompetence and quackery of all save a small minority of the Washington correspondents. This struthion fear of the light is surely not to be noted in any of the actual professions. The medical men, in their trade journals, criticise one another frankly and sharply, and so do

131

the lawyers in theirs: the latter, indeed, are not above taking occasional hacks at the very judges, their lawful fathers and patterns of grace. As for the clergy, every one knows that they devote a large part of their professional energy to refuting and damning their brethren, and that not a few of them do it on public stumps, with the laity invited. So, also, in the fine arts. It is impossible for an architect to affront humanity with a blotch without hearing from other architects, and it is impossible for a poet to print anything at all without tasting the clubs of other poets. Even dramatists, movie actors, chiropractors and politicans criticise one another, and so keep themselves on tiptoe. But not journalists. If a Heywood Broun is exasperated into telling the truth about the manhandling of a Snyder trial, or a Walter Lippmann exposes the imbecility of the Russian "news" in a New York *Times*, or an Oswald Garrison Villard turns his searchlight on a Boston *Herald* or a Washington *Star*, it is a rarity and an indecorum. The organs of the craft—and there are journals for journalists, just as there are doctors for doctors—are all filled with bilge borrowed from Rotary and Kiwanis. Reading them, one gathers the impression that every newspaper proprietor in the United States is a distinguished public figure, and every circulation manager a wizard. The editorial boys, it appears, never fall down on their jobs; they are not only geniuses, but also heroes. Some time ago, having read all such journals assiduously for years, I stopped my subscriptions to them. I found that I preferred the clipsheet of the Methodist Board of Temperance, Prohibition and Public Morals.

But if there is thus little or no frank and open discussion of the evils that beset journalism in the Republic, there is a great deal of private discontent and soul-searching, and it shows itself in all the fantastic codes of ethics that issue from embattled professors of journalism in the great rolling-mills of learning, and from editorial associations in the cow States. . . .

3

In their private communions, though seldom in public, the more conscientious and unhappy variety of journalists commonly blame the woes of the craft upon the entrance into newspaper ownership of such opulent vacuums as Cyrus H. K. Curtis and the late Frank A. Munsey. As a result of the application of chain-store methods to journalism by these amiable Vandals there are fewer papers than there used to be, and the individual journalist is less important. All the multitudinous Hearst papers are substantially identical, and so are all the Scripps-Howard papers, and all the Curtis papers, and so were the Munsey papers in the great days of that pathetic man. There is little room, on the papers of such chains, for the young man who aspires to shine. Two-thirds of their contents are produced in great factories, and what remains is chiefly a highly standardized bilge. In the early days of Hearst, when he had only a few widely-scattered papers, his staffs were manned by men of great professional enterprise and cunning, and some of them became celebrated in the craft, and even generally. But now a Hearst paper, however inflammatory, is no more than a single unit in a long row of filling-stations, and so it tends to attract only the duller and less picturesque sort of men. There is scarcely a Hearst managing editor today who amounts to anything professionally, or is heard of outside his own dung-hill. The platitudes of Brisbane and Dr. Frank Crane serve as pabulum for all of them. What they think is what the machines at the central factory think; what they do is determined by men they have never seen. So with the Scripps-Howard slaves, and the slaves of Cox, and those of Curtis, and all the rest. Their predecessors of a generation ago were gaudy adventurers, experimenters, artists; they themselves are golf-players, which is to say, blanks. They are well paid, but effectively knee-haltered. The rewards of their trade used to come in freedom, opportunity, the incomparable delights of self-expression; now they come in money.

But the sweet goes with the bitter. The newspapers of today, though they may be as rigidly standardized as Uneeda biscuits, are at least solvent: they are no longer the paltry freebooters that they used to be. A Munsey, perhaps, is a jackass, but he is at least honest; no one seriously alleges that his papers are for sale; even the sinister Wall Street powers that Liberals see in the background must get what they want out of him by being polite to him, not by simply sending him orders. The old-timers, contemplating the ghastly spectacle of a New York *Sun* submerged in the Munsey

133

swamp and an *Evening Post* descending from a Villard to a Curtis, forget conveniently how bad most of the papers they once worked for really were. In the town where I began there were five papers, and four of them were cheap, trashy, stupid and corrupt. They all played politics for what there was in it, and leaped obscenely every time an advertiser blew his nose. Every other American city of that era was full of such papers—dreadful little rags, venal, vulnerable and vile. Not a few of them made great pretensions, and were accepted by a naïve public as organs of the enlightenment. Today, I believe, such journalistic street-walkers are very rare. The consolidations that every old-timer deplores have accomplished at least one good thing: they have got the newspapers, in the main, out of the hands of needy men. When orders come from a Curtis or a Munsey today the man who gets them, though he may regard them as ill-advised and even as idiotic, is seldom in any doubt as to their good faith. He may execute them without feeling that he has been made an unwilling party to an ignominious barter. He is not condemned daily to acts whose true purpose he would not dare to put into words, even to himself. His predecessor, I believe, often suffered that dismaying necessity: he seldom had any illusions about the *bona fides* of his boss. It took the whole force of his characteristic sentimentality to make him believe in his paper, and not infrequently even that sentimentality was impotent without the aid of ethyl alcohol.

Thus there is something to be said for the new newspaper Babbitts, as reluctant as every self-respecting journalist must be to say it. And in what is commonly said against them there is not infrequently a certain palpable exaggeration and injustice. Are they responsible for the imbecile editorial policies of their papers, for the grotesque lathering of such mountebanks as Coolidge and Mellon, for the general smugness and lack of intellectual enterprise that pervades American journalism? Perhaps they are. But do they issue orders that their papers shall be printed in blowsy, clumsy English? That they shall stand against every decent thing, and in favor of everything that is meretricious and ignoble? That they shall wallow in trivialities, and manhandle important news? That their view of learning shall be that of a bartender? Has any newspaper proprietor ever issued orders that the funeral orgies of a Harding should be described in the language of a Tennessee revival? Or that helpless men, with the mob against them, should be pursued without fairness, decency or sense? I doubt it. I doubt, even, that the Babbitts turned Greeleys are responsible, in the last analysis, for the political rubbish that fills their papers—the preposterous anointing of Coolidge, the craven yielding to such sinister forces as the Ku Klux Klan and the Anti-Saloon League, the incessant, humorless, degrading hymning of all sorts of rogues and charlatans. The average newspaper proprietor, I suspect, gets nine-tenths of his political ideas from his own men. In other words, he is such an ass that he believes political reporters, and especially his own political reporters. They have, he fancies, wide and confidential sources of information: their wisdom is a function of their prestige as his agents. What they tell him is, in the long run, what he believes, with certain inconsiderable corrections by professionals trying to work him. If only because they have confidential access to him day in and day out, they are able to introduce their own notions into his head. He may have their jobs in his hands, but they have his ears and eyes, so to speak, in theirs.

Even the political garbage that emanates from Washington, and especially from the typewriters of the more eminent and puissant correspondents there resident, is seldom inspired, I am convinced, by orders from the Curtis or Munsey at home: its sources are rather to be sought in the professional deficiencies of the correspondents themselves—a class of men of almost incredible credulity. In other words, they are to be sought, not in the corruption and enslavement of the press, but in the incompetence of the press. The average Washington correspondent, I believe, is honest enough, as honesty goes in the United States, though his willingness to do press work for the National Committees in campaign time and for other highly dubious agencies at other times is not to be forgotten. What ails him mainly is that he is a man without sufficient force of character to resist the blandishments that surround him from the moment he sets foot in Washington. A few men, true enough, resist, and their papers, getting the benefit of it, become notable for their independence and intelligence, but the great majority succumb almost at once. A few months of associating with the gaudy magnificoes of the town, and they pick up its meretricious values, and are unable to distinguish men of sense and dignity from mountebanks. A few clumsy overtures from the

135

White House, and they are rattled and undone. They come in as newspaper men, trained to get the news and eager to get it; they end as tin-horn statesmen, full of dark secrets and unable to write the truth if they tried. Here I spread no scandal and violate no confidence. The facts are familiar to every newspaper man in the United States. A few of the more intelligent managing editors, cynical of ever counteracting the effects of the Washington miasma, seek to evade them by frequently changing their men. But the average managing editor is too stupid to deal with such difficulties. He prints balderdash because he doesn't know how to get anything better—perhaps, in many cases, because he doesn't know that anything better exists. Drenched with propaganda at home, he is quite content to take more propaganda from Washington. It is not that he is dishonest, but that he is stupid—and, being stupid, a coward. The resourcefulness, enterprise and bellicosity that his job demands are simply not in him. He doesn't wear himself out trying to get the news, as romance has it; he slides supinely into the estate and dignity of a golf-player. American journalism suffers from too many golf-players. They swarm in the Washington Press Gallery. They, and not their bosses, are responsible for most of the imbecilities that now afflict their trade.

4

The journalists of the United States will never get rid of those afflictions by putting the blame on Dives, and never by making speeches at one another in annual conventions, and never by drawing up codes of ethics that most of their brethren will infallibly laugh at, as a Congressman laughs at a gentleman. The job before them—that is, before the civilized minority of them—is to purge their trade before they seek to dignify it—to clean house before they paint the roof and raise a flag. Can the thing be done? It not only can be done; it *has* been done. There are at least a dozen newspapers in the United States that already show a determined effort to get out of the old slough. Any managing editor in the land, if he has the will, can carry his own paper with them. He is under no compulsion, save rarely, to employ this or that hand; it is not often that owners, or even business managers, take any interest in that business, save to watch the payroll. Is his paper trifling, ill-informed, petty and unfair? Is its news full of transparent absurdities? Are its editorials ignorant and without sense? Is it written in English full of *clichés* and vulgarities—English that would disgrace a manager of prize-fighters or a county superintendent of schools? Then the fault belongs plainly, not to some remote man, but to the proximate man—to the man who lets such drivel go by. He could get better if he wanted it, you may be sure. There is in all history no record of a newspaper owner who complained because his paper was well-edited. And I know of no business manager who objected when the complaints pouring in upon him, of misrepresentations, invasions of privacy, gross inaccuracies and other such nuisances, began to lighten.

Not a few managing editors, as I say, are moving in the right direction. There has been an appreciable improvement, during the past dozen years, in the general tone of American newspapers. They are still full of preposterous blather, but they are measurably more accurate, I believe, than they used to be, and some of them are better written. A number of them are less absurdly partisan, particularly in the smaller cities. Save in the South and in the remoter fastnesses of New England the old-time party organ has gone out of fashion. In the big cities the faithful hacks of the New York *Tribune* type have begun to vanish. With them has gone the old-time drunken reporter, and in his place is appearing a young fellow of better education, and generally finer metal. The uplifters of the craft try to make him increase, and to that end encourage schools of journalism. But these seminaries, so far, show two palpable defects. On the one hand, they are seldom manned by men of any genuine professional standing, or of any firm notion of what journalism is about. On the other hand, they are nearly all too easy in their requirements for admission. Probably half of them, indeed, are simply refuges for students too stupid to tackle the other professions. They offer snap courses, and they promise quick jobs. The result is that the graduates coming out of them are mainly second-raters—that young men and women issuing from the general arts courses make better journalistic material.

What ails these schools of journalism is that they are not yet professional schools, but simply trade schools. Their like is to be found, not in the schools of medicine and law, but in the institutions that teach barbering, bookkeeping and scenario-writing. Obviously, the remedy for their general failure is to borrow a leaf from the book of the medical men, and weed out the incompetents, not after they have finished, but before they have begun. Twenty-five years ago any yokel who had got through the three R's was free to study medicine in the United States. In three years, and sometimes in two years, he was turned out to practice upon his fellow hinds, and once he had his license it was a practical impossibility to challenge him. But now there is scarcely a medical school in the United States that does not demand a bachelor's degree or its equivalent as a prerequisite to entrance, and the term of study in all of them is four years, and it must be followed by at least one year of hospital service. This reform was not achieved by passing laws against the old hedge schools: it was achieved simply by setting up the competition of good schools. The latter gradually elbowed the former out. Their graduates had immense advantages. They had professional prestige from the moment of their entrance into practice. The public quickly detected the difference between them and their competitors from the surviving hedge schools. Soon the latter began to disintegrate, and now all save a few of them have disappeared. The medical men improved their profession by making it more difficult to become a medical man. Today the thing is a practical impossibility to any young man who is not of genuine intelligence.

But at least two-thirds of the so-called schools of journalism still admit any aspirant who can make shift to read and write. The pedagogues who run them cannot be expected to devote much thought or money to improving them; they are in the position of the quacks who used to run the hedge medical schools. The impulse toward improvement, if it ever comes at all, must come from the profession they presume to serve. Here is a chance for the editorial committees and societies of journalists that now spring up on all sides. Let them abandon their vain effort to frame codes of ethics and devote themselves to the nursery. If they can get together a committee on schools of journalism as wise and as bold as the Council on Medical Education of the American Medical Association they will accomplish more in a few years than they can hope to accomplish with academic codes of ethics in half a century.

All the rest will follow. The old fond theory, still surviving in many a newspaper office, that it is somehow discreditable for a reporter to show any sign of education and culture, that he is most competent and laudable when his intellectual baggage most closely approaches that of a bootlegger—this theory will fall before the competition of novices who have been adequately trained, and have more in their heads than their mere training. Journalism, compared to the other trades of literate men, is surely not unattractive, even today. It is more amusing than the army or the cloth, and it offers a better living at the start than either medicine or the law. There is a career in it for the young man of original mind and forceful personality—a career leading to power and even to a sort of wealth. In point of fact, it has always attracted such young men, else it would be in an even lower state than it is now. It would attract a great many more of them if its public opinion were more favorable to them—if they were less harassed by the commands of professional superiors of no dignity, and the dislike of fellows of no sense. Every time two of them are drawn in they draw another. The problem is to keep them. That is the central problem of journalism in the United States today.

I seem to be in a mood for constructive criticism. Let me add one more pearl of wisdom before I withdraw. I put it in the form of a question. Suppose the shyster lawyers of every town organized a third-rate club, called it the Bar Association, took in any Prohibition agent or precinct politician who could raise the dues, and then announced publicly, from the Courthouse steps, that it represented the whole bar, and that membership in it was an excellent form of insurance—that any member who paid his dues would get very friendly consideration, if he ever got into trouble, from the town's judges and district attorney. And suppose the decent lawyers of the town permitted this preposterous pretension to go unchallenged—and some of them even gave countenance to it by joining the club. How long would the legal profession in that town retain its professional honor and dignity? How many laymen, after two or three years, would have any respect left for *any* lawyer, even a judge

Yet the journalists of the United States permit that precise thing to go on under their noses. In almost every city of the country there is a so-called Press Club, and at least three-fourths of them are exactly like the hypothetical Bar Association that I have described. They are run by newspaper men of the worst type—many of them so incompetent and disreputable that they cannot even get jobs on newspapers. They take the money of all the town grafters and rascals on the pretense that newspaper favors go with its receipt. They are the resorts of idlers and blackmailers. They are nuisances and disgraces. Yet in how many towns have they been put down? In how many towns do the decent newspaper men take any overt action against them? My proposal is very simple. I propose that they be shut up, East, West, North and South, before anything more is said about codes of newspaper ethics.

18

The Case of Hearst

(A review of *Hearst: An American Phenomenon,* by John K. Winkler.
The American Mercury, July 1928)

Mr. Winkler is obviously too light a psychological grappler to get anywhere with Hearst. The man is simply beyond him, as George Washington was beyond Woodrow Wilson. Confronted, for example, by Hearst's recent astounding *volte-face,* whereby Dr. Coolidge has curiously acquired brains and old Andy Mellon has become a sort of Santa Claus, he can only observe humorlessly that "all this would indicate a growing conservatism of thought in an aging man who has vast properties to leave to his sons." The theory, unluckily, is so banal that it fails to satisfy even its author, so he adds, "But I believe these quirks are just evidences of Hearst's bland inconsistency." It would be hard to imagine a schoolboy, or even a schoolmaster, doing worse.

Nor is Mr. Winkler much better when he tackles the other problems presented by the Hearstian psyche. He gives a workman-like objective account of the man, but it never gets beneath the surface. The young Hearst who was expelled from Harvard for a too great exuberance of spirits seems to be quite as mysterious to him as the disintegrating Hearst who snoozes voluptuously beneath his California vine and fig-tree, diverted by the Rotarian

141

platitudes of Polonius Brisbane and the soft gurgle of movie queens. Hearst is sixty-five. It is not, intrinsically, a great age. Men have done good work, and even immortal work, far later in life. But not journalists. Not newspaper men. The roaring Hoe presses grind the life out of even the sturdies long before his kidneys give out. Hearst, professionally, has been moribund for years. What remains of him today is only a caricature of the man who, in the McKinley epoch, made journalistic history.

What he thinks of himself no one will ever know, for he is singularly reticent and even secretive, and men who have worked with him for a quarter of a century seem to be as completely baffled by him as Mr. Winkler. The two men who might have written satisfactory lives of him were Brisbane and Ambrose Bierce. Both have now joined the immortal dead, Bierce biologically and Brisbane spiritually. Bierce, in his last years, professed to hate Hearst powerfully, but all the while it was plain that he also admired him—a capital combination in a biographer. Brisbane, for the sake of posterity, should have quarreled with him ten or fifteen years ago; the result would have been a thrilling book, combining all the virtues of Boswell's *Johnson* and the Bryce report of atrocities in Belgium. But now it is too late, for Brisbane appears to be growing forgetful—so forgetful, in fact, that he has forgotten all the lofty economic and socio-economic principles of his own youth and prime. I observe him applying a vaseline mop to such grotesque heroes as Andy Mellon and the late Judge Elbert H. Gary, and am filled thereby with a vast sadness. For I am growing old myself, and so I can remember when he operated upon fellows of that kind with very different weapons. It was a gaudy era, and, for one, I greatly enjoyed living in it.

The central fact about Hearst, I venture to suggest, is that there has always been far more innocence in him than guile—that he remains at sixty-five, as he was when he singed the whiskers of Pulitzer, a goatish and unsubtle college boy, eager only to have a hell of a time. Whoever tries to read any rationality into his journalistic theory will end with a dizzy ringing in the ears. There was no sense in his support of Bryan in 1896: it was simply a device to inflame Mousterian Man and give Pulitzer to sweat. Bryan himself, though designed by God to be fooled always, quickly got the measure of it and departed from the Hearstian embrace, his

Bible clutched to his breast. Nor was there any sense in Hearst's riotous brewing of war medicine in 1898—that is, journalistically— for the war cost him a great deal more than he got out of it, both in money and in prestige. He whooped it up simply because he was full of malicious animal magnetism, and eager for a bawdy show. Mr. Winkler tells how vastly he enjoyed his own modest share in the carnage. The only Spaniards he actually encountered were disarmed and half scared to death, but he leaped upon them with fearful hosannas and took them prisoner in the best manner of his own special commissioners.

His political career, now unhappily closed, was one long record of surprises and imbecilities. He got into politics by a sort of accident, and continued in a purely sportive spirit. It was often hard to determine which side he was on, and what he advocated. His cabinet of advisers consisted mainly of newspaper reporters trained in his own city-rooms: no doubt it amused him to observe how easy it was for these amateurs to alarm the professionals. Al Smith, who takes politics seriously, distrusted him from the start, and finally declared war to the death upon him. The history of his Independence League deserves to be written: I herewith commend the job to Frank R. Kent. This so-called party was simply a gigantic bladder attached to a string, and with it Hearst battered the heads of all the professional politicians. Life must have been extremely pleasant for him in those days: if he did not laugh himself to sleep every night, then I overestimate his intelligence. At St. Louis, in 1904, he actually came within reach of the Democratic Presidential nomination. If the bluff of Alton B. Parker had been called, the convention might very well have turned to him. It would have been a colossal campaign: Hearst vs. Roosevelt. The two men had many things in common, but what they mainly had in common was their boyish delight in uproar, their naïve lust to make sensations. Naturally enough, they became bitter enemies, and Roosevelt spent his last years denouncing Hearst. But he learnt more from Hearst, first and last, than he learnt from any other man save P. T. Barnum. At one time in his career at least a half of his policies were borrowed from the chromatic headlines of the New York *Evening Journal.*

I suspect that Hearst's taste for violent rough-house survives to this day, but of late he has shown a lamentable falling-off in his old high ingenuity and enterprise. He really passed from the scene when the new tabloids began to break up his monopoly on dime-novel news. He should have invented the tabloid himself; it is a wonder, indeed, that he didn't do it twenty-five years ago. As it was, the onslaught of the *Daily News* and the *Graphic* caught him at a bad time. He was trying to reorganize his business and cut down his losses, and the Huns were within his citadel before he knew it. By the time he came into action it was too late; his imitation tabloids were failures, and some time ago he sold them to the Hon. Alexander P. Moore, L.L.D., Ambassador to Peru and relict of Lillian Russell. The transaction was mysterious, and is still the subject of suspicion in newspaper offices. The episode of the forged Mexican documents brought Hearst out of his California retirement, but only transiently, and, I am bound to add, ridiculously. The old steam was simply not there. The business was handled clumsily, and its net issue only called painful attention to the rustiness of the Hearst machine. Evidently there are no more Sam Chamberlains, Karl Deckers or James Creelmans in the *Evening Journal* office. A genuine Hearst paper cannot be run by bookkeepers; it demands men of action, with lush and florid imaginations.

Hearst deserves more and better of his country than he will ever get. It is the fashion to speak of him contemptuously, with dark references to matters that are nobody's business. I think there is a great deal of envy in all this: not many Americans, even among millionaires, have ever been accused so beautifully. The dislike of the man that prevails in newspaper circles is only a smarting of old wounds. He shook journalism to its foundations, and exposed the incompetence of more than one highly smug newspaper proprietor. They were all imitating him by 1900, and they all show the marks of his teeth to this day. American journalism before his time was extremely ponderous and platitudinous. Even Pulitzer greatly fancied himself as a publicist, and showed plain traces of the messianic delusion. Even the old *Sun* labored under a sense of responsibility to the Flag and the Truth. Hearst upset all that by parodying it. He made a burlesque of the whole God-save-us scheme of things. He proved that what the populace really wanted was simply a roaring show—and he brought to the business of giving it that show a resourcefulness that was unparalleled and a

144

daring that was stupendous. It was quite impossible for the old-fashioned papers to stand up to him; they had to follow him or perish. Thus he set them all to whooping and bawling, and the net result was a rapid decline in their old authority. The proletariat, taken to a palpable circus, became cynical, and it remains so to this day. Nothing remains sacred to it. It is still exploited, to be sure, but it no longer worships its exploiters. In 1895 the Sunday-school scholars of the land were yet being taught to venerate such heroes as Commodore Vanderbilt. Today that adoration is confined to a small caste of humorless fanatics—bishops, Washington correspondents, Rotarians.

Hearst is probably the only rich man ever heard of in America who has really had a good time. Harvard tried hard to tame him, but failed dismally. The blood of adventurers ran in him, and he had a restless and iconoclastic soul. Instead of wasting his money upon hospitals and libraries and going in for social climbing, he poured his millions into yellow journals, and was presently enjoying all the thrills of a mad King. The populace swarmed after him; the politicians began to fawn over him; the money barons trembled at his name. Wasn't that better than playing golf? Wasn't it better than becoming an overseer of Harvard? Wasn't it better than acting as banker to Elder Hays? I think it was. I believe that Hearst got his money's worth, and that he doesn't regret the cost today. That he was deceived, now and then, by his own buncombe, is probable: it is the human way. But he was not deceived very often. It was the show that kept him going, not any brummagem sense of duty. He reduced all solemn and highfalutin things, including especially patriotism, to a common level of clowning. In other words, he reduced them to their actual content of truth. I believe his career has been a very useful one, despite his obvious deficiencies. Cant is still the curse of America, but it is not quite the curse that it used to be. Today even Hearst himself cannot pump any dignity into Andy Mellon.

19

Georgia Twilight

(Baltimore *Evening Sun,* December 30, 1929)

Three years ago, in 1926, Julian Harris, editor of the Columbus (Ga.) *Enquirer-Sun* received the Pulitzer Prize for "the most disinterested and meritorious public service rendered by an American newspaper during the year." It was, in journalistic circles, a very popular award—far more popular, indeed, than most of the others that the Pulitzer trustees have made. Mr. Harris and his wife, Julia Collier Harris, had taken over the *Enquirer-Sun* in 1923, and under great difficulties had made it one of the best small dailies, not only in the South but in the whole United States. Its policies were courageous and civilized, and its editorial page was always diverting and often brilliant.

Now I look at that same editorial page, of a day taken at random. The leading editorial deals heavily with the news that but 27 percent of the male morons at the University of Georgia want what is described as "culture" in their wives. The runner-up is a banal discussion of Dr. Hoover's proposal that food-ships be permitted to pass unmolested in war time. The third and last editorial gurgles over the fact that a Georgia boy won a prize in the Dixie section of the Atwater-Kent radio contest. So much for the views of the

146

editor. Next door to them he runs an article by Bugs Baer, and under it a quotation from the Bible. There follow two news items—one announcing the destruction of a still, and the other giving next Sunday's sermon topic at the First Baptist Church of Columbus. The rest of the page is given over to a boiler-plate cartoon, a report of the meeting of a Methodist missionary society at Midland, Ga., a couple of paragraphs of Army orders, and an installment of a maudlin serial called "Cotton Stockings," by one Alma Sioux Scarberry.

Needless to say, the Harrises are no longer responsible for the paper. Last August control of it passed to Charles Marsh of Austin, Texas, and J. M. Stein, of Brownsville in the same State, a pair of chain-store newspaper owners in those parts. It was announced then that the Harrises were to stay, but that soon turned out to be untrue. On November 2 Mrs. Harris was dismissed from the staff, and a short while later Mr. Harris resigned. Now the paper is wholly in the hands of Stein, Marsh, Bugs Baer and company.

II

Its passing, following so soon after the like passing of the Columbia (S.C.) *Record,* is a heavy blow to decent journalism in the South, for it has been, for half a dozen years past, a sort of beacon and guide-post to scores of lesser papers. What Harris did so bravely and effectively in Columbus the more aspiring of the little country editors of Georgia and the adjacent States tried to do in their own towns, and often with considerable success. He taught them how to write plainly and he showed them that it was possible to live in the South and still think clearly. Thus the *Enquirer-Sun* acquired a string of disciples, and the journalism of the region began to look up.

Harris's leadership, of course, was due primarily to his own high professional competence. He not only had vastly wider experience of the world than most Southern journalists; he was also a naturally bellicose and pertinacious man. No conceivable labor, however arduous, could stay him, and no opposition, however furious, could daunt him. But he also had something else, and that

147

was a name that was as honorable in Georgia as the name of Lee in Virginia. He was the son of Joel Chandler Harris—and the son of Joel Chandler Harris could not be easily disposed of. It was impossible to dismiss him loftily as a Damyankee, or as a spy of the Pope, or as a Bolshevik.

So Harris plugged away, damning seriatim all the frauds and fakes who afflicted the South, and especially Georgia—the Ku Kluxers, the Anti-Saloon League blacklegs, the lynching Baptists, the witch-burning Methodists, and the whole sorry company. He took aim at the middle of their foreheads, and he plumped them every time. There were howls in all directions, but presently there was heard too a scattering of applause. It increased as year followed year. Columbus is a mill-town, but there are plenty of people in it who are civilized, and they began to be very proud of the *Enquirer-Sun*. It was talked about all over the South. It brought in a kind of publicity that Rotary and Kiwanis, for all their hard striving, could not match. And when the award of the Pulitzer Prize showed that the North, too, had begun to take notice, there was general rejoicing.

III

But meanwhile Harris had begun to find his labors too much for one man. He was not only the editor of the *Enquirer-Sun*, with ten or twelve hours of heavy labor before him every day; he was also the business manager. In both offices he got diligent and very effective help from Mrs. Harris, but naturally their chief interest lay in the editorial room, and so the business affairs of the paper began to suffer. Perhaps Harris was not really a business man at all: journalists of his type seldom are. Whatever the fact, he eventually found himself in difficulties, and so the offer of Stein and Marsh to take over half his troubles seemed almost providential.

But Stein and Marsh, it appears, do not admire the type of paper that such a man as Harris produces. They seem to have little interest in leading public opinion, scotching frauds, putting down abuses and outrages; their aim is to get out safe and fat little papers that no one will ever object to—sweet, juicy, dumb little papers

148

that please everyone, and especially everyone with something to sell. They have a string of such papers in the backwaters of the South, and now they have another one in the *Enquirer-Sun.* Having got rid of the Harrises and put in reliable hacks of their own, they will soon begin to make money. And then, I daresay, they will be happy, and maybe even proud.

This, of course, is a philosophy like any other, but I confess that it is hard for me to understand it. What fun can it be to print a paper which prints Bugs Baer, "Cotton Stockings" and the news of the local Baptist tabernacle on its editorial page, and devotes itself to congratulating the winner of the Atwater-Kent contest, Dixie section? How can any rational man get anything resembling satisfaction out of writing editorials for such a sheet? I can't answer, but there are men who can, and some of them prosper greatly in journalism.

IV

Where the Harrises will land I don't know, but no doubt there is still room for them in Southern journalism; certainly it needs them very badly. In Columbus their departure has caused an uproar, and the women's clubs and other such agencies are busily passing resolutions of protest. My hope is that they will find posts in some larger town than Columbus—not because it was inhospitable to them, for it wasn't, but because their effectiveness would be increased by having more mass and weight behind them. What they did in Columbus, with business worries consuming them, they could do ten times as well in Atlanta or Birmingham, with plenty of money in the till.

The two of them, husband and wife, are perfectly matched. Both write very charmingly, and yet they know how to call things by their right names. Their private interests are those of persons who have travelled a good deal, and had interesting adventures. They read the good books, they are devoted to the fine arts, and they do not neglect the art of good living. Mrs. Harris is the complete antithesis of the usual lady journalist: she stands as far from the sob sister as she stands from the W.C.T.U. virago. She can do literally anything that a daily newspaper needs to be done. As for

Harris, he is a sound professor of all the journalistic arts and crafts. With equal facility and the same furious energy he can cover a hanging or write a blistering editorial.

The adventure of the pair in Columbus is surely not to be set down a failure. It was really a grand success. Starting with next to nothing, and in the face of cruel and incessant difficulties, they left their mark upon the journalism of the South. They have put heart into many a young man whose work remains to be done. They will be heard about for a long while. For they have made the kind of fight that is not easily forgotten.

20

Twenty Years

(Baltimore *Evening Sun,* April 21, 1930)

I

The denunciations of itself that *The Evening Sun* printed on Friday last, in celebration of its twentieth anniversary, were mainly so good-humored that it would be ungrateful to discuss them seriously; nevertheless, it is probably fair to accept them as representative of the general view of the town. In that general view it is certainly impossible to detect anything properly describable as pride. There are plenty of Baltimoreans who seem to be proud that the General Electric Company is building a plant here, and bringing in 30,000 more morons to man it, or that the Bethlehem Steel Company is enlarging its stink-pots and doubling its smoke, or that this or that other great corporation, chased out of Harrison, N. J., or Newport News, Va., by the advance of civilization, is preparing to move here, but so far as I can make out there are precious few who get any satisfaction out of the thought that the town has developed two very unusual newspapers, and that both are great successes.

Here, I hope, I may speak with good grace, for though I have been a contributor to one of these papers, off and on, since its first issue, I am in no wise responsible for its policies, and seem to have less influence in shaping them, in truth, than the office boy. I can recall but one case for a year past in which any suggestion that I made was adopted, and in that case it was a very obvious one, and would have certainly occurred to some one else within twenty-four hours. During the first six of the twenty years that I have served *The Evening Sun* I devoted myself to criticizing it daily, sometimes in harsh terms, and for ten years past I have protested in season and out of season against the flippancy which some of its friends complained of on Friday.

But the fact remains that, in the face of great difficulties, it has somehow made itself a really distinguished newspaper, as such things do in the United States, and that, along with its ma, the *Sunpaper,* it has got itself talked of all over the world. When I travel, which is not infrequently, I am constantly colliding with that somewhat curious fact. The two *Sunpapers* are known everywhere, both in Europe and in America, and the general view of them, especially among newspaper men, seems to be very high. This is especially true in England, where I lately had the honor of suffering. No other provincial American newspaper is so well esteemed there, either by journalists or by public men, as the *Sunpaper,* and of the metropolitan papers only two, the *Times* and the *World,* are so well known.

II

The sources of this reputation, I suppose, are to be sought in the independence of the two papers, and in the unusual character of their news services. Most American newspapers, in late years, have tended to clump into chains, and so they have generally lost character and personality. What is printed by one is printed by ten, thirty or a hundred others. Save for a few home-made banalities, the same news is in all of them, and the same editorials, and the same features. Thus they move toward a flashy puerility, for what is published in Boston or Chicago must be something that is also acceptable in Memphis and Akron. How far this standardization has gone is but little realized by the average reader, for he seldom sees any papers save those of his own town. But every newspaper man knows that it is almost complete, and that it greatly diminishes the interest and dignity of his trade.

The two *Sunpapers,* like the Chicago *Tribune* and the New York

Herald Tribune, stand clear of this Fordization. For good or for evil, they are their own men, and can afford to take their own line. They are controlled, as to ownership, by Baltimoreans; they have no entanglements either with political aspirants or with other newspapers; and their staffs enjoy a degree of autonomy that is probably unmatched in American journalism. Thus they are free to print the truth as they see it, both in their news columns and on their editorial pages, and that, in fact, is what they do day in and day out, as I can testify who have often disputed their truth, and not infrequently disproved it.

Such complete freedom, it seems to me, is of the essence of sound journalism. It makes for enterprise in news-gathering, for there is no *a priori* assumption against any fact that may happen to be hauled in, and it makes for an unusual frankness in editorial discussion, for there is no external compulsion to take any particular line, and what is argued today may be abandoned, if it appears to lose validity, tomorrow. Best of all, it makes for a generally liberal and intelligent case of mind, for liberalism is obviously a function of freedom, and cannot exist without it. It is for these reasons that the better sort of journalists favor independent papers, and that their prevailing view, both at home and abroad, is friendly to the two *Sunpapers.*

III

But this professional view, though it is probably sound, is not shared by many laymen. Their attitude toward public affairs, if only because they have little time to devote to the subject, tends to be highly conventionalized and unyielding, and so they usually prefer platitudes to facts. What the precise truth is about something not actually under their noses does not greatly interest them; they are content to accept any explanation that is simple, and so puts no burden upon their minds. Thus they seldom differentiate between careful and accurate news reporting and the ordinary guff, and when they notice a difference they are very apt to prefer the latter to the former.

No doubt this fact is responsible for the general feeling in Baltimore, especially among men of the more respectable sort, that the two *Sunpapers* are somehow disturbing, and perhaps not quite moral. I suspect that it originated in the years immediately after the Armistice, when the elder *Sunpaper* was slowly getting together its staff of foreign correspondents, now incomparable in American journalism. Those correspondents were carefully selected, and the corps gradually came to include some of the most eminent journalists of Europe. Its contributions to the paper were immensely valuable, and they had a very palpable effect upon the more enlightened men, content to accept the Creel Press Bureau view of the war and most such men, I daresay, are still inclined to regard them with suspicion.

The Evening Sun has not gone in much for foreign news, but it has spent a great deal of energy and money trying to report accurately and interpret rationally the affairs of the nation, and like its ma it has upset thereby the equanimity of many worthy Baltimorons. Both its excellent Washington correspondence, from Mr. Henry M. Hyde and his colleagues, and its editorial comments have made war upon the comfortable assumption that the United States is run by great and good men; they have revealed a vast array of asses, and an even vaster array of rogues. Such revelations do not soothe men whose security is bound up with the existing order, and it is only human nature that they should dismiss the disquieting as false, perverse and in bad taste.

IV

No one has asked me for my opinion, but God inspires me to enter a few caveats of my own. The senior *Sunpaper,* it seems to me, continues to suffer, almost like its chief critics, from the war psychosis: it devotes too much attention to what is going on in Europe and too little to what is going on here at home. The fact that Baltimore is a great city, roaring with life, is scarcely apparent from its pages. It deals competently with official local matters, but that is as far as it goes. I believe that the question why a shad fish for which a fisherman in the bay gets 30 cents costs $2.50 in the Baltimore markets is far more interesting and far more important than the question why Italy wants eight battleships instead of seven. . . .

As for *The Evening Sun,* I agree . . . that it diminishes its

authority by taking too light a view of the national clown-show. . . .
I can see nothing amusing in the fact that Dr. Hoover, in order to
promote his chances of reelection in 1932, has appointed a hireling
of the Anti-Saloon League to the Federal bench. It seems to me
that such malfeasance in office is inordinately disgraceful and
disgusting, and that it ought to be denounced in plain terms. (In
that denunciation, I believe, the few remaining decent men on the
Federal bench ought to join, if only by resigning what has ceased to
be an honorable office.) And I believe that *The Evening Sun,* like
the *Sunpaper,* covers Baltimore in a wooden and uninspired
manner, and misses much that people are talking about.

As I say, no one has asked for my views. Moreover, my
experience in the past has not convinced me that they are desired.
So perhaps I had better shut up and shut down.

21

Journalism in the United States

(Literarische Echo [Berlin], May 11, 1931)

Successful newspapers are common in the United States, but good ones are almost as rare there as they are in England. There are whole areas of the country, as large as most European states, in which the standards of journalism are as low as one might reasonably look for in the most remote and backward provincial town. Consider, for example, the so-called New England group of states—Maine, Massachusetts, New Hampshire, Vermont, Connecticut and Rhode Island. It has an area of 66,415 square miles— more than a third that of Germany—and a population of 8,166,341 —more than that of Sweden or Holland. And yet there are but two decent newspapers in the whole of it—the Springfield *Republican* and the Portland *Evening News,* both of them in small and unimportant cities. In Boston, the center of a metropolitan area of more than 1,000,000 population, there is not a single newspaper of even the second class. Its people read sheets made up mainly of gossip about suburban social events—weddings, church choir concerts, birthday parties, and so on. Only one of them ever prints correspondence from Europe—and that one is the organ of the Christian Scientists, and refuses to notice deaths and disasters!

Some of the largest cities in America are equally bare of decent newspapers—for example, Philadelphia, with a population of nearly 2,000,000, Detroit, Pittsburgh and Los Angeles. There was a time, long ago, when Philadelphia had intelligent and influential papers, but that time is no more. Its principal journal today, the *Evening Bulletin,* has a large circulation and makes a huge profit annually, but it is so badly written as to be almost illiterate, and nothing even remotely resembling an idea ever appears in it. So in Detroit. The chief paper there, the *Free Press,* is simply the mouthpiece of the town Babbitts. It is not only indifferent to every form of intelligence; it is actively hostile. So again in Pittsburgh and Los Angeles, not to mention Washington, Denver, Minneapolis, Buffalo, Cincinnati, Seattle—an almost endless list. The chief newspaper of Los Angeles for long maintained—I believe, still maintains—a "health" column conducted, not by medical men, but by quacks. And one of the principal Chicago papers made its salient contribution to American thought in the form of a department of astrology—a feature that has since been imitated by scores of other papers.

It may be thought by Germans that this frank catering to the mob causes such papers to take a radical line in politics, but this is by no means the case. On the contrary, the most vulgar sheets are usually the most conservative, for the mob in America is itself conservative. At the time of the Sacco-Vanzetti uproar there were very few protests against the execution of the two men from American workers; in general, the business had the approval of the proletariat, if only on the ground that Sacco and Vanzetti were foreigners. By American law, of course, a foreigner has a few rights, though surely not many; but in the popular view he has none whatever. Thus the American working classes commonly read and support very reactionary papers, and there is, indeed, but one radical paper printed in English in the whole country—the Milwaukee *Leader,* which belongs to the right wing of the Socialists, and is certainly not extremist.

Of Liberal papers representing the thought of the more enlightened *bourgeoisie* there are several, but they are printed in such places that they cannot exert much influence upon the nation as a whole. The only one of general circulation, the New York *World,* recently suspended publication, destroyed by the double competi-

157

tion of the vile tabloids which devote themselves to crime, and have no politics, and of the ultra-conservative mouthpieces of Big Business. There remain, in the big cities, only the Cleveland *Press,* the St. Louis *Post-Dispatch,* and the Baltimore *Sun.* All these, by some accident of fate, remain prosperous, and all labor hard to keep a civilized spirit alive in their communities.

The Baltimore *Sun* is probably the most important of the three. It maintains correspondents in the European capitals, covers the United States very thoroughly, and has the exclusive right, in America, to the dispatches of the Manchester *Guardian,* the traditional organ of English Liberalism. Its territory is small, but it is published only 40 miles from Washington, and so it reaches the chief politicians of the country, sometimes with excellent effect.

The St. Louis *Post-Dispatch,* which is owned by the same publisher family which published the deceased New York *World,* is not much read outside of St. Louis, but there it has a large and appreciative audience and a considerable influence. St. Louis was mainly settled by Germans, and the founder of the *Post-Dispatch,* Joseph Pulitzer, began his career by publishing a paper in the German language. He came to the United States full of the spirit of '48, and that spirit is still visible in the *Post-Dispatch.* It pays relatively little attention to European affairs, but it is very active in unearthing and exposing corruption in the United States and has a staff of highly competent reporters. Its editorial position is always enlightened, and its political writing is graceful and persuasive.

The most successful of American newspapers, in all probability, is the New York *Times.* It is an incredibly dull and stodgy journal, but it spends immense sums for special dispatches, and so its news service, though not always unbiased, is thorough. It prints all public documents in full, and also reports at length the speeches and other pronunciamentos of the chief national wizards. Thus persons who wish to learn the last sickening detail of the news have to read it. The task is a formidable one, for it discourages agreeable writing. Its editorial views are those of Wall Street. So are those of its chief rival, the New York *Herald Tribune.* But the *Herald Tribune* employs competent writers for its news columns, and even its editorials, of late, have shown a certain liveliness. Some time ago it began the policy of attracting Liberals to its staff. Its first victim was Lewis S. Gannett, one of the editors of the Liberal weekly, the *Nation.* Its second was Walter Lippmann, late editor of the defunct New York *World.* More are said to be marked for capture. So far these Liberals have not dissuaded the *Herald Tribune* from its fundamental conservatism, but, as I have said, it has begun to grow a bit lively, and so there is hope.

Not many of the provincial newspapers of the United States discuss public affairs with any intelligence. Most of them simply repeat what the local bankers and businessmen say at the local country clubs. The most enlightened political writing is to be found in the three Liberal weeklies, the *Nation,* the *New Republic* and the *New Freeman.* The *New Freeman,* as I write, is changing itself into a monthly, for the rich Liberal who backs it (I believe he is a German-American) has tired of the weekly deficits. It will probably disappear altogether before very long. The *New Republic,* which made a great splash when it first appeared, now grows rather dull, and is not read as much as it used to be. This leaves the better part of the field to the *Nation,* whose editor, Oswald Garrison Villard, is the son of a German '48er.

Villard, whose family name was originally Hilgard, is a man of great energy and positive ideas, and no American journalist has ever served his country better. He is a man of large means, but he has made the *Nation* pay its way. It is constantly deluded and disappointed by politicians who pretend to be Liberals, but it never loses either hope or steam. The American conservatives hate it with a consuming hatred, but many of the ideas it advocates one year are forced upon them the next. It has been a brave and sturdy opponent of American imperialism and of the Fascism that flourishes at home, and no victim of oppression ever appeals to it without getting help. Villard used to edit a daily paper, the New York *Evening Post.* It is a pity that he is not editing one now.

22

Tainted News

(A review of *Mobilizing for Chaos*, by O.W. Riegel.
The Yale Review, December 1934)

It is just two hundred years since John Peter Zenger won his memorable battle for the freedom of the press in America: the occasion is thus a meet one for printing Dean Riegel's gloomy report upon the state of that freedom today, here and elsewhere. On all sides it appears to be in rapid decay. There are still, to be sure, countries in which there is no overt censorship, and the United States is one of them, but everywhere the news is heavily polluted by official propaganda, and everywhere the means of transmitting it tend to come under government control, which is to say, under the control of politicians. Are our own telegraph wires free? For the present, yes—but the Brain Trust is already scheming to take them over. In all save a few small areas of Europe they fall as far short of complete freedom as the American mails. As for the cables and the radio channels, they are free hardly anywhere, even in name.

Mr. Riegel has a great deal that is interesting and instructive to say about the press associations. We think of them, in this country, as great agencies for the distribution of impartial news, and it must be admitted that at home they make a hard effort to live up to that character. But when it comes to news from abroad they encounter formidable difficulties, for in large part they must depend upon the foreign agencies, practically all of which have propaganda purposes, and when they attempt to go it alone they are easily and frequently impeded by official contriving. What the difficulties amount to in practice was shown during the last years of Machado's bloody rule in Cuba, when the choice was between taking his word for it or sending out no news at all, and again in Germany at the time of the Nazi purge, when nothing issued from Berlin for days on end save a mixture of palpably untruthful communiques from the Wilhelmstrasse and romantic speculations from the Adlon bar.

Nor is home news always beyond suspicion, despite the laudable professional diligence of those told off to gather it. They have, ordinarily, little confidence in official announcements, but very often there is nothing else to go on. This is especially true in Washington, where the concealment and sophistication of news are carried on in the grand manner, and the number of news sources is so enormous that no staff of correspondents, however large, could conceivably cover all of them, or undertake a careful scrutiny of the bulletins of those covered. The thing goes even further, for Washington has now learned how to bring pressure on the home offices. This was done with little attempt at concealment in the autumn of 1933. Every American newspaper that ventured to report the prodigies of the New Deal realistically was accused of seeking to nullify its boons, particularly in the field of child labor, and many were intimidated into totalitarian acquiescence.

Mr. Riegel has put together an impressive record, and his comments upon it are sound and sensible. As he shows, the corruption of news is mainly in the hands of nationalistic politicians, and their purpose everywhere is to array nation against nation. They are thus preparing the way for another war. It might be prevented if they could be overthrown, for people in general have little interest in their neighbors, and would not cherish hatreds if they were let alone. But getting rid of these warlocks involves solving a long series of problems that still baffle human ingenuity. As things stand, turning out one gang is often only a preliminary to installing a worse.

161

23

Twenty-Five Years

(Baltimore *Evening Sun*, April 15, 1935)

I

It would be natural, I suppose, to say that the day when *The Evening Sun* was hatched seems only yesterday, but if I were on oath it would certainly be perjury, or something else of like wickedness and the same name. The truth is that, as I look back upon the birthday of this great moral organ, it appears infinitely remote in time, and very vague in outline. I simply can't remember what happened; it was a day like any other. We got out the first issue without any of the pangs and dubieties that seem to be proper on such occasions. We knew in advance that it was going to be bad, and it *was* bad, so we put it out of our minds as quickly as possible. Later on, I am glad to add, the paper improved.

I became a member of the staff by a sort of accident, and never had any recognized office or title. I had come to the *Sunpaper* in 1906 when the *Evening Herald,* of which I was editor, succumbed, and for three years I enjoyed the placid and lordly life of a *Sun* man under the Abell regime. There was never on this earth a more pleasant newspaper office. It was full of charming fellows, and the Abells carried it on as if it were a good club rather than a great industrial plant. I began as Sunday editor, but by 1910 I was writing editorials.

Then came Charles H. Grasty, an apparition from a strange planet. I knew him, but had reason for believing that he didn't like me, so I prepared to shuffle on. But he sent me word that he had no intention of canning me, whereupon I consented coyly to stay, and in a little while we were very friendly. It wasn't long before he began to make plans for an evening edition. Inasmuch as I was one of the few men in the editorial rooms who had had any experience on an evening paper, I was naturally taken into his councils, and when the paper came out at last, on April 18, 1910, I found myself a sort of first mate to J.H. Adams, the editor.

II

My duties, at the start, were rather complicated. I was supposed to be at my desk at 8 o'clock every morning, and to write two editorials before 11 o'clock. In addition, I had to read all the letters received from correspondents, and to translate into English those that seemed suitable for *The Evening Sun* Forum. If any nuts came in with proposals for new laws or unearthly schemes to beat Taft in 1912, I usually had to listen to them for Adams was busy in his cage, damning the telephone and trying to write his own leaders. If he was still busy at 11:30 I made up the editorial page for him. Then to the Rennert for lunch.

Of an afternoon I devoted myself to a long signed article for the next day. It was printed in the column next to the editorials, and was set in such crowded type that it consumed a great many words. When I undertook this job it seemed easy enough, for I was busting with ideas in those days, and eager to work them off. But in a little while I found that writing 2,000 or 3,000 words a day was really a killing chore, and one day I remember especially, when sitting at the typewriter became suddenly unendurable, and I turned to pen and ink for relief.

When Adams found me using such paleozoic implements he was horrified, and, with his usual decency, let me off some of the editorial writing. But soon after that his health began to be indifferent, and he was sometimes disabled, and at such times I had to do a double stint. I don't remember ever having a disagreement with him, though the only thing we had in common, politically speaking, was our belief in the Bill of Rights. But rows are very rare in newspaper offices. Men of all sorts of ideas somehow manage to get along together.

One rather curious incident of our association I recall. At the end of a busy afternoon Adams called me into his office and asked me to find out what I could about airships. "It looks to me," he said, "as if they were actually coming in, and we ought to have somebody in the place who knows something about them. You are a graduate of the Polytechnic, and should be able to find out how they work." I agreed to do it, but had to report my failure a few weeks later. To this day my knowledge of airships is precisely nil. I never see one in the air without expecting it to fall.

III

How long my job lasted I don't remember exactly, but it wasn't very long. By the end of 1910 I was transferred to the last column of the editorial page, and turned loose upon the town under the style and appellation of The Free Lance, and there I performed daily for five years, with only two intervals out for brief trips abroad. This work was a lot of fun, but it brought me so many visitors and so much mail that editorial writing on the side became impossible, and I have never done any since.

I apologize for talking so much more about myself than about *The Evening Sun*. My share in it, in fact, has always been small, and since its first days I have given a good part of my time to other enterprises. But a newspaper man always thinks of his paper in terms of his own job, and that must be my excuse. Some of these days, I hope, the history of this one will be told in more or less detail. It will be a story of a hard and long fight against depressing odds, carried on with magnificent devotion by a gang of strictly non-messianic and very amusing fellows, and ending in an extraordinary success.

The changes that have come over American journalism during the twenty-five years of *The Evening Sun* have been marked and many, and nearly all of them, it seems to me, have been for the good. There are old-timers who pine for the days when every considerable American city had eight or ten newspapers, but I am not one of them. The truth is that the majority of those newspapers were shabby rags that printed very little news, and fell far below the chastity proper to Caesar's wife. They overworked and underpaid their men, and were constantly blowing up. That their treadmills produced some extremely competent journalists is a fact, but it is also a fact that they polluted the craft with a great many shady quacks.

IV

In my early days, I confess, some of these quacks enchanted me, for the romance of journalism—and to a youngster, in that era, it surely *was* romantic—had me by the ear, and the quacks themselves, in many cases, were picturesque characters, and not without a certain cadaverous glow. But chance threw me, when I was still in my early twenties, into the post of city editor, and as such I had to get out a paper with their aid. The experience convinced me that the newspaper business was in need of a wholesale disinfection, and I am glad to be able to say that it came anon, and has left apparently permanent good effects.

The improvement in newspapers has been general, and very great. Their machinery for gathering news is enormously better than it was when I was a young recruit. More news now comes into the *Sunpaper* office every night than came into it in two weeks back in 1900, and that news is better written and more accurate. It is almost impossible today for an event of any significance to be missed, but in my nonage it happened every day. The New York *Sun* was, in many ways, the best of the American papers a generation ago, but it had only the most meager news service, and at the time of the San Francisco earthquake, in 1906, it came out with nothing save a few brief bulletins and a fine obituary of the town of Will Irwin, written in the office.

Newspapers are a great deal more honest than they used to be, and a great deal more intelligent. Some of the Stone Age editorial writers survive in legend as masters of prose and publicists of the first chop, but the truth is that most of them were only third-rate rhetoricians itching for public office. Nothing that any of them wrote, on public questions, whether in their papers or elsewhere, is worth reading today, or is remembered by anyone. Even the prose of William Cullen Bryant, perhaps the most respectable of them, is ... deadly and ... dead. ...

The improvement in newspapers I ascribe mainly to the increased cost of operating them. When a new one could be set up by any adventurer with a hand press and a few cases of type, the trade naturally attracted a great many dubious persons, and their competition kept even the best papers on a low level. But the invention of the linotype made large capital investments necessary, and in a little while the weaker and more vulnerable sheets began to disappear. Those papers that survive today, whatever their faults otherwise, are at least safely solvent, and they show the virtues that always go with solvency, that is to say, they are not purchasable, they spend money freely in discharging their public responsibilities, they stand aloof from the corruptions of party politics, and they are able to attract to their service a well-educated and self-respecting corps of men. Here, as in so many other fields, capitalism shames the mountebanks who deride it.

24

Speech to the Associated Press

(New York, April 20, 1936)

Mr. President, Ladies and Gentlemen:

There is probably no younger man on earth, either in outward aspect or interior fire, than Mr. Frank B. Noyes, and yet the sworn records show that he has been president of the Associated Press for 36 years. Dizzy years indeed, and full of revolutions. I am allowed only three hours for my sermon this afternoon, so I can't rehearse all the changes that have gone on, but there is at least time to mention a few of them. When Mr. Noyes took office as the head of this little club there was not, in all the world, a jazz band, a radio crooner or a movie star. Nearly a million veterans of the Civil War were still alive, and only a few hardy pioneers had ever had their tonsils cut out. McKinley was president, Henry Ford had just quit a nice job with the Detroit Edison Company and was being laughed at for trying to build automobiles, and the first flight of an airship was three years off. Men flocked into theatres to see women's legs, and women sneaked into department stores, blushing and looking back over their shoulders, to buy powder-puffs. Here in New York Prohibition was heard of only as a far-off and incredible hobgoblin, like the Dalai Lama, or cannibalism.

167

It was about the time Mr. Noyes became president that I saw my first piece of A.P. copy. It was a small sheet of flimsy, reporting that some eminent criminal had been hanged—maybe ten lines, no more. Not a word from the lawyers. No interviews with the wives or spiritual advisers of the deceased. Even the name of the hangman wasn't mentioned. The whole thing might have been engraved on a ten-cent piece. It went on page 4, which was about equal to page 37 today, and got a spot pretty far down the page. No art . . .

Certainly we have seen a lot of progress since that primitive era. What the full A.P. report now amounts to on a busy night I don't know precisely, and neither, I suppose, does anyone else, not even Kent Cooper. All I am sure of is that, down in the Baltimore *Sun* office, it is now common to get more news from Kitzmiller, Maryland, or Omsk, Siberia, than we used to get from New York or Sing-Sing. The sporting department alone occupies more space, works more men and uses more different kinds of type than the whole news section of thirty-six years ago. Taking all the American dailies together, they print more stuff about a good juicy murder than their predecessors of 1861-65 printed about the entire Civil War. Lindbergh's clipping-book is four times as thick as George Washington's. When the President makes a speech we not only print it in full; we also print a two-column summary of it, a summary of the summary in a ten-point lead, and a summary of the summary of the summary in a first-page box.

But it isn't only in news-gathering that the newspapers of the United States have forged ahead. They have also made enormous progress in art and beautiful letters. I well remember how, as a young Sunday editor, I had to concoct my own colored comics. First I had to find an idea that hadn't been used for at least two weeks, then I had to find an artist sober enough to make the drawings, and then I had to see them through the engraving and stereotying departments and the press-room. If the blue eye of a redfaced character got anywhere within the limits of his face, we called it good register. But now there are great factories turning out comic mats by the bale, and they print as beautifully as banknotes and are full of the same nourishing boloney. The column boys do almost as well for literature. Some time ago a colleague told me that he had counted no less than 18 columns in one issue of a New York paper. I got a copy and counted 19: another columnist had been put to work between the 7 A.M. noon edition and the 1 P.M. absolutely last final, with closing stock-market quotations. That night I read all 19 columns. Nine of them were devoted to denouncing the other ten. The other ten, I should add in justice, were free from this vituperation. Their authors gave over all their space to stroking and scratching themselves.

But now, having recalled some of our triumphs in our chosen art, I hope I'll be forgiven for mentioning our grandest and gaudiest failure. I allude, of course, to the editorial page. It has been going downhill steadily for fifty years. No one thinks of great American editors anymore; everyone thinks of great sports writers, comic artists and columnists. Yet it seems to me—and in fact I admit it in a whisper as one who has performed principally on editorial pages for a generation past—that no other page on the newspaper of today is better manned. It enlists good men, and sometimes brilliant men, and they work hard and faithfully. On even the worst paper, the editorial page offers the best stuff on tap in the office. It shows more careful writing than any other page, and not infrequently it shows wider information, and sounder judgment.

Yet how many read it and heed it? If you want to find out, call in your best editorial writer when you get home, feed him some gunpowder and blood, and sit him down to write a scathing editorial on any subject you fancy. Then print it on your editorial page. You will get a few letters, and a few of your local bores will call up—no more. But then take exactly the same editorial and reprint it next day on your *first* page, in type suitable for that hot spot, and with appropriate headlines. If you get less than ten times as many letters, call me up in Baltimore with charges reversed, and a case of Maryland rye will be at your disposal. Every bore within a radius of a hundred miles will be down on you, you will be expelled from half your clubs, and if luck is really with you, you may even land in jail.

Why are such effects impossible on the editorial page? They are impossible for several plain reasons. One is that the editorial page, save in a few newspapers, is so gloomy and forbidding, typographically, that only a reader itching for punishment is ever tempted to read it. It prints the longest paragraphs in the paper and under the smallest heads. It is mainly written and made up before anything actually happens, and at least half the time what it says about things that happened yesterday is blown up by the follow-ups of today. If you printed college yells under such feeble one-line heads they would sound like algebraic equations.

There is something else. The effort to keep the news columns clean of editorializing has reacted on the editorial page itself. We have all worked so hard—and no one less than the directors of the Associated Press—to make news-writing really impartial that we have come near making editorial-writing impartial too. Is that an improvement? I begin to have some doubt of it. The first job of a newspaper, to be sure, is to print the news, and nowhere on earth is it done more diligently or more honestly than in this great free Republic, the envy and despair of all the decadent principalities of Europe. But printing the bare news is only half of that job. The rest is interpreting it, showing what it signifies, getting some sense and coherence into it.

In brief, the newspaper is not only a news-monger; it is also a critic. That it may be a bad one is beside the point; nine-tenths of all critics are bad ones. The essential thing is that it is the only critical agency of any genuine competence and influence that is left in the American scheme of things. The pedagogues of the country, when they became public jobholders, cut their own throats—as many of them now begin to realize. No one pays any attention to them any more; when they are heard of at all it is as comic characters. The pulpit has gone further and fared worse: in most communities it is now tolerated only in so far as it confines itself to post-mortem matters, and never says anything that can be either proved or disproved. The halls of legislation hardly deserve to be mentioned at all. The only actual division of opinion that they ever show is over the question whether A or B should have the job. The Opposition in the English House of Commons is a living force, and, as we saw only lately, is really able to influence government policy. But in Congress the minority has no rights that the majority is bound to respect. When it is knocked in the head it is forbidden even to howl.

This leaves the field open to the newspapers of the country. They constitute its only effective opposition, and one of their clearest duties is to keep a wary eye on the gentlemen who operate this great nation, and only too often slip into the assumption that they own it. I don't argue here that newspapers ought always to be agin'

170

the government. Far from it. All I argue is that they ought to be ready for it when, as and if it needs attention. And when they have something to say about it, whether in challenge or in commendation, they ought to say that something in type legible at a distance of at least six inches, and under headlines suitable to the importance of the subject, and in a place less depressing than the funeral parlor of the editorial page.

I ameliorate my heresy by hastening to add in conclusion that the editorial page . . . (without such criticism) would still have the function of offering useful information and refined entertainment to the more philosophical type of reader. It could go on printing such things as I have long contributed to it myself—learned, delicate essays which strike a neat balance between pro and con, and leave only the sweet sound of music on the ear. But when there is really something to be said, why not say it where people will hear it. Why go down into the cellar to hold an auction sale—and selling ideas is an auction sale precisely like any other? Why not get out on the sidewalk, and ring a bell?

25

The Public Prints

(Baltimore *Evening Sun,* December 14, 1936)

I

Some time ago the *Evening Sunpaper* reprinted in this place a long tirade by the *Christian Century,* a politico-theological weekly published in Chicago, against the daily newspapers of the Republic. Its substance was that they were full of hellment, and sworn enemies of the only true righteousness. In proof thereof the *Christian Century* recited a long list of their torts, including especially the atheistic sneers that some of them levelled, in the late campaign, against the inspired Munyons of the New Deal. In their opposition to those Munyons, so we were told, "they flung to the winds the canons of fair, responsible, sportsmanlike journalism," and delivered over not only their editorial columns but also their news columns "to partisan propaganda, much of it false."

With all due respect to the *Christian Century*'s pious editor, Brother Charles C. Morrison, D.D., Litt.D., LL.D., bosh! He is an ingenious but far from ingenuous man. On the one hand, it is not true, as he argued, that "80 percent of the daily newspaper circulation in the nation" was flung against the New Deal. On the other hand, it is not true that their war upon it was carried on in a violent and unfair manner. And the third hand, so to speak,

Brother Morrison very neatly omits from his indictment his own chief count against the newspapers, and the chief count of every other politico of the ghostly faculty, to wit, their long, vigorous and, in the end, melodramatically successful assault upon Prohibition.

In brief, the late drys are still rubbing their wounds, and every time the excuse offers to bite their conquerors they do so with alacrity. In all this lush and lovely land there is probably not a single Prohibitionist who believes that the wet press was really honest. Each and every one of them, touring the dismal Sunday-schools behind the railroad tracks, continues to hint that the papers were bought by the Beer Trust, the Whiskey Trust, the Yellow Chartreuse Trust, the Green Chartreuse Trust, the Graacher Himmelreich Trust, and all the rest of the Gomorran monsters of those almost forgotten days. It was the wicked journalists' fierce bellowing against the Anti-Saloon League that really upset the faculty, not by any means their relatively polite and *pianissimo* booing of the Brain Trust.

II

The legend that the combat against the Hon. Mr. Roosevelt and his associated mountebanks was carried on in an extravagant and inordinate manner is now fostered chiefly by the Communists and their fantoddish allies. They made precisely the same charges that Brother Morrison makes, and fly equally wide of the facts. The truth is that nearly all the really furious invective of the campaign came from the other side. I know of no anti-Roosevelt newspaper in the country, not even the Chicago *Tribune*, that went as far in violence and abuse as the Stern and Scripps-Howard papers went on the other side, and I know of no individual journalist, not even the lamentably non-constructive Frank R. Kent, who bawled and beat his breast in the manner of such humorless More Abundant Lifers as Heywood Broun, A.B. (Harvard), president of the "I Am Not a Communist, But"—Association.

The New Deal won so handsomely, indeed, mainly because those who were opposed to it went beyond the bounds of discreet strategy in being fair to it. Very few of the opposition newspapers

173

tackled it in their news columns. Most of them printed the news of the campaign with complete impartiality, and most of that news was naturally favorable to the administration, for the administration had control of the news-making machinery, and was aided by far more skillful propagandists than the opposition could muster. During one week of the campaign—I think it was in early October —I examined and listed all the campaign news on the first three pages of the *Sunpaper.* No less than three-fourths of it emanated from administration sources, and was definitely pro-administration in tendency.

All the principal newspapers of the country have been trying hard, for years past, to keep their editorial opinions out of their news columns, and many of them have so far succeeded that anything which supports them now has difficulty getting into print. This leaves them only their editorial pages, for the work of illumination and persuasion—and American editorial pages, as every newspaper man knows, have been dead for thirty years. What is printed on them is so little regarded by the majority of readers that every smart editor—for example, the naughty Hearst —moves his show to the front page whenever he really has anything to say.

III

It is not true, as Brother Morrison and the Communists allege, that eighty percent of the daily newspaper circulation in the United States was against the Hon. Mr. Roosevelt in the late campaign. This was the case, to be sure, in a few big cities, but it was certainly not the case generally. It is a fact, however, that more papers were against him than were for him, and it is also a fact that among the former were most of the journals of any ponderable reputation for honesty and good sense. There were exceptions here, but they were not many.

Why, then, did the Hon. Mr. Roosevelt win so gaudy a triumph? Part of the answer I have already indicated: the better the paper, the fairer it is to opponents, and in this instance the opposition grabbed everything it could get. But there is something more, and it has to do with the peculiar psychology of mobs. They are forever running amuck, first this way and then that, and arresting their motion is a long and difficult business, requiring not only great industry and patience but also a considerable skill at demagogy. Every election since the World War, not only in this country but in all other democratic countries, has been a landslide, and some of those landslides have been far more impressive than the one that lodged Dr. Roosevelt in the White House for four more years.

The history of such landslides is always the same. A pressure group of some kind or other—sometimes it is moral or theological, but more often it is simply political—forces a new and crazy idea upon the dull rogues who constitute the government of the nation, and once they have adopted it they put all the weight of official propaganda behind it. Thus the mob is converted to it, and is presently in such a frenzy of enthusiasm that all dissent becomes a kind of treason. There ensues the slow, painful process of debamboozlement. It takes years, and is full of grief for those who undertake to further it. But in the end it succeeds—and the mob leaps to some fresh lunacy.

IV

In the present case the business is following classical lines. The New Deal came in on the heels of departing Prohibition, just as Prohibition came in as the paranoia of wartime oozed out. Prohibition, in its fourth year, seemed forever unbeatable, and in its eighth year it looked almost the same. But in its tenth year it began to crack, and in its thirteenth year it blew up with a bang. As it was cleared off the New Deal took its place, and the whole dismal process began all over again.

How long it will take to get rid of the New Deal I do not profess to know, but certainly the job will not be a short or easy one. It will not be so much as begun until the more enlightened newspapers of the country devise some means of overcoming the official propaganda, now so overwhelming. The same sort of propaganda swamped them during the first years of Prohibition, but eventually they managed to throw it off, and after that the dry hellenium had an increasingly hostile press, and toward the end it was hammered by virtually all the decent newspapers of the country, day in and day out. Whether or not this will happen in the case of the New Deal remains to be seen, but unless and until it does happen the quacks at Washington, barring acts of God, will be safe.

Their downfall can never be brought about by academic denunciations of them on editorial pages, for editorial pages have become as occult and repulsive to the mob as the works of Immanuel Kant. The mob is not insusceptible to argumentation, but that argumentation must be of the sort that it is used to hearing from politicians, evangelists, charity mongers, auctioneers and other such whoopers. That is to say, it must be of the sort that appeals powerfully to the emotions, and to the emotions only. But even such argument has its limitations, for its very vehemence makes it quickly wearisome. The way to sway people in the mass, whether of the lower orders or the higher, is to have at them with multitudes of cogent and dramatic facts, appealing directly to their self-interest. The New Deal will be doomed the day the newspapers of the country cease to fill their columns with official propaganda in favor of it, and devote their space to the laborious amassing of the truth about it.

26

Speech to the American Society of Newspaper Editors

(Washington, D.C., April 6, 1937)

Any discussion of the situation of the American editorial page had better start with a fundamental question, to wit, Why should anyone read it at all? I must confess that, in looking over some of the pages now current, I find it impossible to imagine any sound reason.

The pull of the other pages is plain enough. The news pages, in the midst of a great deal of bosh and tosh, usually give the reader the essentials of the day's news, and news is something that all human beings crave, at all times and everywhere. Moreover, virtually all human beings crave the same kind. You will hear prigs protesting against the printing, say, of crime news, but it always turns out on cross-examination that they never miss reading it. A hanging is a good story to an archbishop just as it is to a street-railway curve-greaser, and so is all the melodrama that precedes it.

The feature pages are almost as popular; indeed, in some papers they are more popular. The reason is not far to seek. They are aimed frankly at the actual tastes of the normal reader. They feed his (and especially her) vanity. They provide plenty of gossip and scandal, sometimes malicious. They are full of the puerile and inaccurate information of public questions by persons especially chosen for their fluent imbecility, which is to say, by columnists, of whom I have long had the honor to be one. Thus they meet a genuine need of readers who have gone through the intellectual shambles of the public schools, and it is no wonder that they are so popular.

The editorial page—by which I mean the section of actual editorials—meets no such need. It is, basically, an attempt to subject public questions to logical analysis—and logical analysis is something that nine human beings out of ten are incapable of and hence uninterested in. Their thinking is not done by that process. They have ideas, to be sure, and some of those ideas are furiously maintained, but they are not reached by syllogism; they are reached by desire and appetite, by yen and libido. At the time President Roosevelt launched his proposal for pulling the fangs of the Supreme Court certain newspapers sent reporters on the streets to find out what the plain people thought of it. The answers, in the main, were divided into two classes, neither of which showed anything more than simple feeling. The majority answered: "I am in favor of anything that Roosevelt wants." The rest answered: "I am against anything that Roosevelt is in favor of."

But while this was going on the editorial writers were filling their space with long and learned discussions of the matter, going back to history and heavy with subtle argumentation. The theory, I take it, was (and is) that there is a public eager for genuine light and leading. In all probability, such a public actually exists. It may be very small, but no doubt a thorough search of any American community would reveal it. But why, if it is real, should it give any serious consideration to anonymous editorials? Why should it follow wizards it doesn't know, whose qualifications it has no means of testing, and whose very convictions are often open to reasonable question?

I hope no one will think that I am here attempting to run down editorial writers. My belief is that there are many smart fellows among them, and the somewhat alarmed respect for them that I picked up in my early reportorial days still survives, though I have since been one myself, and have even hired and fired them. When I was a magazine editor I got a great deal of excellent stuff out of them, often to their own surprise. It amazed them to discover how well they could write, and what good ideas they had, once they had thrown off their false faces, and begun to function as their own men. Some of them liked it so well that they quit their jobs and set up as independent publicists, and some of the some are making fairish livings at that trade to this day.

But how can any man be expected to do really effective writing under the conditions they commonly face? Only too often they must write at high speed, and with insufficient preparation, and at all times they must give primary consideration, not to what they may happen to think or feel themselves, but to what some higher functionary thinks or feels. And when that higher functionary himself does the actual writing, he is not uncommonly incommoded by trying to figure out, not what is the truth, but what is consistent with the paper's character, or past performance, or future plans, or what will please some still higher functionary.

All these allegations have been made against newspaper editorial writing by lay critics, and sometimes they have been resented hotly, as if they impugned the honor of newspapers. But all of us know that they are generally true—if not on all newspapers, then at least on a great many. The job of the editorial writer is actually almost hopeless. He is expected to achieve effects under such cruel handicaps that they would cripple a writer of the first class, working with both arms free. Deprived of the chief strength of any writer—the force and color, such as they are, of his own personality—he carries on his art like a surgeon wearing boxing-gloves or an actor with a wooden leg.

Is there any remedy for his disease—any way to liberate him? Maybe not, but we can at least speculate. If I were the sole editor and proprietor of a newspaper, which God forbid, I think I'd start off by abolishing the editorial page as it now stands. It fails to interest the majority of readers and it fails to persuade the minority. It is a vestigial organ, and most of its old functions have now passed to the columnists and headline writers. It wastes a lot of excellent brain-power, and costs a lot more than it is worth, either to the paper or to the common good.

The first thing to do, it seems to me, is to let the editorial writers appear in their own persons, and the second thing is to take them off dealing with all things briefly and superficially and to put them to dealing with a few things thoroughly and at length. The notion

179

that people won't read long articles is nonsense. Those who can really read at all will read an acre—if it is well done. Many editorial writers, in my experience, know a great deal about this or that. If they had more elbow room they could set it forth much more persuasively than they do now, and if they did it over their own names they would take much more pains to set it forth charmingly.

Would the great masses of the plain people read them and heed them? Probably not. But that is only saying what I have said already—that the great masses are shy of logic, and can be reached only by appeals to their feelings. That appeal can never be made by intellectual devices. It must be made by the arts of the showman. I see no reason why a newspaper, in seeking to put over an idea, should not make use of the expedients already in use by its advertisers, and even by its feature writers. That is, I see no reason why it should not employ illustrations for the purpose, and vociferous typography, and the style of the radio fireside chat, the auction sale and the college yell. The primary object of public argumentation is not to show off the argufier's elegance; it is to set the customer to panting, sweating and beating his breast. That can never be done by putting the thing into small type, and under one line heads.

The objection that any such hullabaloo would destroy the impartiality of the news columns is of very little force. The news columns are not actually impartial now, and they probably never can be. Those of you who argued against the New Deal in the last campaign—and so vainly—should know what I mean. While you were setting off your squibs on your editorial pages, your front pages roared with New Deal propaganda, most of it supplied at the cost of the taxpayer you were professedly trying to succor, but not a little of it concocted by your own men.

The tremendous development of this propaganda in late years has seriously corrupted the news. A great deal of it has become, in its raw state, only a kind of ballyhoo. I'll give you two examples, and then shut down. The first is provided by the proceedings of the LaFollette investigating committee. For weeks on end it filled the first pages with evidence that some of the larger employers of the country were setting spies upon their working people, fomenting disorders, and otherwise carrying on in an anti-social manner. This was important news, and it deserved to be printed. But not once during the whole uproar was there any hint that there had been any provocation from the other side. The employers were represented as mere criminals, and not a word was said about the forays and extortions that had scared them in the first place, and set them to doing the silly and brutal things that scared men always do.

The second example is less glaring but almost as significant. Last February the Department of Superintendence of the National Education Association was meeting at New Orleans. There were thousands of gogues in attendance, and they devoted a week to discussing the problems of their trade. What they said and did got very little space in the newspapers, and perhaps deserved even less. But on February 21 thirty of them put their heads together and sent a telegram to the White House, whooping up the raid on the Supreme Court. In one great paper that I could mention that telegram got a swell spot on Page 1, and then jumped to nearly a column on Page 2, with a full list of signers at the end. No one in the office seemed to notice that only thirty had signed out of more than 3,000 in attendance, that the telegram had been prepared by two professional radicals, and that it no more represented the general opinion of the assembled gogues than it did that of the Supreme Court itself.

I am not arguing that this telegram should have been ignored. It was actually, in its way, news, though certainly not important news. All I am arguing is that printing it without a gloss, like printing the LaFollette testimony without a gloss, was plainly misleading. In controversial matters the news can never be one side only; it must be both sides. It seems to me that the American newspapers, in the face of the immense propaganda now flooding them, have forgotten or neglected that capital fact. In an effort to let everyone be heard they have given all the advantage to the most vocal and enterprising side. They will never be doing their duty until they invent some way to strike a better balance. They will not be printing the true news until they show what is behind every effort to corrupt it.

But here I wander off into the news-room, which is not my present theme. The editorial-room, to return to it, is a much sadder sight. Its brave lads are trying to sweep back an ocean with brooms. Worse, they diligently avoid big brooms, and use only tiny little ones. Yet worse, every sweeper is blindfolded and knee-haltered before he begins, and confined to a few square feet of the shore. No wonder the waves roll in.

27

A Note on News

(Baltimore *Evening Sun*, May 10, 1937)

I

Newspaper men like to think of news as something wholly objective, but it can be so only under exceptional circumstances. In its ordinary forms it is not merely a statement of overt facts; it is some concrete individual's opinion of the truth and significance of those facts. He may try in all honesty to keep his customary prejudices out of it, but nine times out of ten they creep in, nevertheless. Send a reporter to a hanging, and if he has any intelligence at all he will get into his account of it some hint of his opinion about the guilt or innocence of the gentleman bumped off. And he will be stupid indeed if he does not add what amounts to a technical criticism of the work of the hangman, the chaplain, and the other officiating dignitaries.

It is, in truth, this admixture of opinion which gives good reporting all its savor. The minutes of Congress include all the essential facts about its proceedings, but no one wants to read them in that form: they are too dull, and what is more, they are largely unintelligible. What the reader wants is not only a report of what went on, but also an interpretation of it. If the reporter in the gallery is a good one, he produces a clear and vivid picture of the show. He does so by getting his own view of it into his report, and by illuminating that report with whatever wisdom he may have at his command.

Most really good news is dramatic, and hence involves a conflict of some sort or other. The well-trained reporter is supposed to maintain neutrality between the combatant parties, but he can do so only up to a point. He is certain, in most cases, to believe that one side is appreciably more virtuous than the other, and when he writes his report that belief inevitably gets into it. At the Hauptmann trial the majority of reporters were early convinced that Hauptmann was guilty, and thereafter their reports gave him the worst of it. Even the press association correspondents, long trained in impartiality and sworn to it in all good faith, showed something of that leaning. In a sense, of course, this was unfair to Hauptmann. But those reporters were not working for Hauptmann, but for their readers, and their readers wanted to be told, not only what actually happened at the trial, but how it struck men on the spot. And whether they wanted it or not, that was what they were bound to get.

II

A good reporter, of course, seldom gives a conscious color to his report. He knows that he is there to discover and publish the truth, not to make argument. But the definition of the truth differs among reporters as much as it does among other men, and in consequence every one of them is thrown back, soon or late, on his habitual attitudes of mind. He can see only through his own eyes, and he can weigh conflicting evidence only in the balance of his own judgment. That judgment may be better in some men than in others, but in none is it completely unbiased.

It is conditioned by a multitude of influences, some of them almost irresistible. There is, primarily, the influence of congenital philosophies. Every Englishman, said W. S. Gilbert, is born either a Liberal or a Conservative. This is, again, the powerful effect of schooling, and of the worldly experience that runs parallel with it. Finally, there is the tremendous effect of everyday associations—

of the ties of friendship and common interest, of customary wont and habit.

The reporter succumbs to these pulls just as every other man succumbs. He picks up, gradually and mainly unconsciously, the point of view of the sort of men he meets every day. If he is a Washington correspondent he is very apt to identify himself with a given group of statesmen, or with statesmanship in general, and so give less time and thought to getting the news than to trying to figure out its possible public effects. And if he has daily truck with politicians lower down the scale it is very easy for him to slip into their way of looking at things, and to measure their acts by their own standards.

Every good reporter tries to combat this influence of the here and now, but surmounting it is not easy. Schemes to help him are not unheard of in newspaper offices, and some of them show a considerable ingenuity. Men are switched from one job to another, and exposed deliberately to counter-influences. The aged *Sunpaper* guards its London correspondents, of whom it is justly proud, by giving them very short tours of duty. None is ever kept in London more than two years. If they lingered longer they would inevitably pick up an English point of view, and so lose something of their value to a patriotic American newspaper.

III

The effect of environment on even the best reporters was exhibited dramatically, and even somewhat amusingly, a few weeks ago, at the time of the battle for the little town of Guernica in Spain. The first news of that battle came from correspondents on the so-called Loyalist side, all of whom were dependent upon Loyalist communiques for their daily information, and most of whom were naturally under the influence of the Loyalist point of view. They reported categorically that Guernica had been destroyed by a fleet of German bombers, and that hundreds of non-combatants had been deliberately murdered. They added that this astounding crime was wholly without military excuse or effect.

When the dispatches thus sent out got back to Spain, and

reached the Insurgent headquarters, the reporters attached thereto were informed that the story was false. Guernica, they were told, had not been bombed at all; it had been set afire by the retreating Loyalists, who hoped thus to hinder the Insurgent advance. These reporters were invited to go to the town and see for themselves. They went in a body, and reported the next day that they could find no sign of a mass bombardment. The place looked, they said, as if it had been set afire. The houses were reduced to bare walls, but there were very few holes in those walls, and all the other signs of an air attack were lacking.

This report, in its turn, soon reached the Loyalist side. But did it convince the reporters there that they had been fooled? It did not. Most of them stuck to their guns. One of them—a very competent and reputable fellow—even went to the length of framing a theory to account for what his colleagues on the other side had sent out as the evidence of their own eyes. Before they were taken to Guernica, he suggested in all seriousness, the Insurgents had rounded up a squad of stone-masons and had the bomb-holes in the walls repaired!

IV

Here, remember, we were not confronted by young and callow reporters, fresh from the seminaries of journalism. The man who swallowed the Loyalist tale were all men of experience, and most of them had been through the World War. The one who concocted the fantastic theory about the stone-masons was the representative of two rich, powerful and honest papers—the *Times* of London and the *Times* of New York. It would be impossible to challenge his good faith. Yet he so far succumbed to the influences surrounding him that he burdened the cables with what it is very hard to distinguish from nonsense.

One can only seek refuge in the resigned reflection that journalism, as yet, is far from an exact science. In controversial matters, the most that a newspaper can hope to do is to present both sides fairly. But even in this direction the going is sometimes difficult. The press-agents employed by the two sides are not likely to stop with the overt facts as they see them; they are very apt to add a great deal of imaginative embellishment. And the journalists told off to report and interpret them only too often end as converts to their hooey.

In the days before Hitler took the throne in Berlin the *Sunpapers* had two correspondents there. One of them was an ardent Hitlerite, and the other was as violently on the other side. Thus the *Sunpapers* printed two series of polemics, both of which probably missed the truth. When Hitler came in his opponent became converted to his gospel, and his former partisan began to denounce him. In despair the *Sunpapers* gave up, and has had no correspondent in Berlin since.

28

The Newspaper Guild

(Unpublished. Written for the *Evening Sun* on August 7, 1937)

I

That the interests of capital and labor are not always identical has come to be generally suspected, and indeed widely believed. That there may be some conflict also between the interests of labor and those of professional labor leaders is less obvious, but evidence of it is surely not lacking. What was accomplished for actual working men by the Hon. John L. Lewis's late effort to inflict his panting will to power on Little Steel? Nothing whatever. A few men were killed, many more had their heads broken, and a vast army lost four or five weeks' wages. The survivors are back at work on substantially the old terms, with the Hon. Tom Girdler and his blacklegs triumphant.

Much the same sort of thing is now going on in the narrower and less homicidal field of journalism, a science which I have infested and glorified for thirty-eight consecutive years, and may thus be presumed to know fairly well. Two movements are proceeding within it. The first is a movement of working newspaper men to reduce their hours of work, improve their pay, and protect themselves against the forays of the predatory Babbitts who control only too many of the American newspapers. The second is a movement by professional messiahs, mainly of indifferent rank and dignity in the craft, to convert the first movement into a grandiose political uprising, by Moscow out of the New Deal, and so transform themselves into a new Brain Trust, with all the high powers and prerogatives that go therewith.

As I write it is not certain how this effort will end. A referendum has been called, and it may be that a majority of the present members of the American Newspaper Guild will have sense enough to clean out the jitney Lewises and Stalins, resume the proper business of their organization, and press hard for its original program. But that this will happen is by no means certain, for in newspaper organizations, as in others on the present imperfect earth, fools tend to make up in numbers what they lack in discretion. If they prevail in the Newspaper Guild, then it will be wrecked, for nearly all its best members will depart, unwilling to be yoked by their inferiors. And even if the fools and their tinpot heroes lose, the organization will have suffered severely from the combat, and its enemies will be greatly encouraged.

II

What it proposed to do, judging it by its original program, is not new, but only greatly overdue. There has been need for years for some rational organization of newspaper men, devoted to improving the condition of the craft. In my time in it the scale of pay has been at least tripled, and on the better newspapers of the country the men have come to be treated with a decent regard for their comfort, security and *amour propre*. But there are still plenty of newspapers on which they are badly used, and even on the better newspapers their rights have been unsufficiently defined.

Perhaps my own experience may throw some light upon this last. I have never, since the first time in 1899, had to ask for a job, and I have never been fired or had my pay reduced. But on two separate occasions during those 38 years, papers on which I worked have been sold out over my head, and I have been left to scratch for myself. Both times, perhaps by the personal intervention of Satan,

I got better jobs at once— but both times I might very well have been left on the beach, with maybe a family to support or some other heavy obligation on my hands.

There is something grossly unfair about this, and not only unfair but also indecent. A newspaper man of any experience and skill is not a mere hired hand, to be taken on or laid off at will. He devoted himself, not to journalism in general but to one newspaper in particular, and if he is really worth his salary he earns appreciably more than it ever comes to. As he reaches the higher ranks the dignity of the paper he works for depends on his character and ability quite as much as it depends on the genius of its proprietors. When they have hired good men they have done the most they can for their property, and the less they harass those good men thereafter the more successfully it will be carried on.

III

Plainly enough, men of this sort cannot flit facilely from paper to paper. Their professional armamentaria have been adapted to the uses of particular employers, and it may be difficult if not impossible for them to find others who need them or want them. The same thing is often true of men lower down the scale. It is, to be sure, an old saying in newspaper offices that when a paper blows up the reporters get new jobs much quicker than the editors, but plenty of reporters are also one-paper men, and some of them are so valuable as to be almost unreplaceable.

Yet all such men, in the past, have lacked any well-defined certainty of status or tenure. The proprietor who paid them was free at any time to sell his paper over their heads, and leave them to their fate. Their staff superiors could discharge them for any reason or no reason at all. Each bargained for his pay on his own, and only too often the better pay went to the better bargainer rather than to the better man. Against the common calamities of life they had no security, for, save on a few papers, the general rule was that when their work stopped their pay stopped.

It was to seek some way out of this unhappy state of affairs that the American Newspaper Guild was organized. There was nothing revolutionary on its agenda. It asked (a) that men discharged for no fault of their own be given reasonable indemnities proportioned to their length of service, (b) that after a sufficient apprenticeship all men alike be paid at least a living wage, suitable to their station and responsibility, (c) that excessive hours be reduced and too scanty holidays lengthened, (d) that provision be made to care for men disabled by illness or accident, (e) that on matters affecting all hands there be free and open bargaining, with the men represented by any spokesman they chose to elect, and (f) that these arrangements be embodied in formal agreements, subscribed to by both sides.

IV

This series of proposals, so far as I am aware, did not cause the responsible executives of any reputable American newspaper to telegraph for Pinkertons or lay in tear-gas. Most such executives were professional newspaper men themselves, and all of them were well aware that what their staffs had in mind was equitable and reasonable. On more than one important paper virtually everything that was asked for was already in effect, and in some directions and on some papers it was actually exceeded.

But this program was no sooner formulated than it began to be transformed into a caricature of itself, growing ever more extravagant and ridiculous. The more intelligent newspaper men, having no great appetite for listening to speeches, went to no meeting that they could avoid and so the show was left to the inevitable messiahs and their dupes. They not only popped up in every considerable town; there also developed a formidable body of professionals radiating out of New York, and everywhere.

Few if any of these professionals were of any consequence in their trade. They came out of the ranks of the chronically oppressed and discontented—the sorry malcontents who hate their jobs and their betters. Some were swallowers of the Moscow buncombs, which is to say, jackasses. Others were pinks of the "I am not a Communist, but—" variety, which is to say, jackasses doubly damned. All were inflamed by the melodramatic fulminations of the Hon. John L. Lewis, and eager to get aboard a bandwagon that promised to flatten out all wicked bosses like pancakes, and provide swell jobs for gentlemen tired of work and eager to alarm the world.

V

Once these starry eyed evangelists were on the bridge the Guild began to make heavy weather. Office boys were taken in to swell the *bloc* of safe and docile votes, and plans were launched to proceed to business office clerks, subscription solicitors, truck-drivers, janitors, and even newsboys. Alliances were made with longshoremen, sailors, bricklayers and other such literati. Weak papers were confronted with demands that would have wrecked them, and punished with siege and riot when they resisted.

Finally, the evangelists and their stooges held a convention at St. Louis in June, and gave away the show. The Guild was pledged to join the Hon. Mr. Lewis in all his schemes, however extravagant; to root for the Spanish Communists, and to support the Hon. Mr. Roosevelt's court-packing plan, and urged to engage in a long list of other great moral enterprises, some of them only silly but others almost insane. It is on these fantastic ventures, none of them having any imaginable relation to the welfare of genuine newspaper men, that the members are now voting by referendum.

If the verdict is no, the Guild will be delivered from the pinks, and restored to a national purpose and usefulness. If it is yes, then every self-respecting newspaper man will kiss it good-bye.

29

Memo to Paul Patterson

(Sometime in 1937)

The primary aim of the *Sunpapers*, both in their news columns and on their editorial pages, must be simply and solely to tell the truth.

That aim is not to be attained by printing what every other paper prints. The ordinary flow of news is partial in two senses. It covers the field inadequately, and a large part of it is launched by persons with private interests to further. Not infrequently those private interests are adroitly disguised as public interests, but their real character remains. We must try to penetrate them and to counteract them. We must detect the falsities, whether of fact or of inference, in the news they launch, and set beside that news a kind that is more realistic and reliable.

At the present time that effort is especially necessary, for we confront a high development of government propaganda in both domestic and foreign affairs. Very little news emanating from Washington, even when it comes through our own bureau, is without bias, and very little news coming from Europe. It should be our fixed policy to be very suspicious of what is generally said and generally believed, and to set forth, whenever possible, the other side. We should bear in mind such facts as these: that H. M. Brailsford, considering his private politics, would be in favor of the Spanish government even if it were clearly wrong, and that all the congressional committees now functioning are looking for ammunition against capitalism, not for the truth about both capital and labor.

A lot may be accomplished by simply presenting the facts, but not everything. Some effort must be made to show their significance, and to expose the motives and methods of those who seek to sophisticate them. In other words, we must make some appeal to the sense of fair play, and even to the self-interest of readers. We'll get nowhere so long as we try to counteract a wholesale and highly skillful playing on the emotions with nothing more formidable than a resort to reasoning.

As for our general policy, I think it should be anti-Administration at all times. It has been so generally since the White Paper, and it brings the power of sound information and impartial honesty against the immense effects of government propaganda, with its constant appeals to the lowest credulities of the people, and its playing on their tendency to believe in and even to worship conspicuous public officials. I do not propose that we denounce the Administration incessantly and unreasonably; I only propose that we view it skeptically, and refuse to assent to its devices and pretensions until we are sure that they are intelligent and sincere. Every public official with large powers in his hands should be held in suspicion until he proves his case, and we should keep him at all times in a glare of light. The fact, say, that Henry Wallace failed miserably and ignominiously at his own private business is a fact of capital importance, and it should be recalled often enough to keep it in the public mind.

At the time the *Sunpapers* were rehabilitated many of the persons chosen to man them, especially on the side of the foreign service, were of Liberal politics. Some of these persons have since become radicals. I believe that the safe and rational course for the papers themselves is still that of Liberalism, and that we should be watchful of radical propaganda by our own men. We should fight resolutely at all times for the chief Liberal goods, all of them well tested and of the highest value, e.g., the limitation of governmental powers, economy in all the public services, complete publicity, the greatest tolerable degree of free speech, and a press secure against official pressure. There is nothing for a decent newspaper in radicalism. If it ever succeeds in this country our function will be gone, and with it our liberties. They will be gone equally whether the radicalism that comes in is of the Right or of the Left.

30

On False News

(Baltimore *Sunday Sun,* September 17, 1939)

In one day last week I encountered the following items of news in the local newspapers:

A dispatch from London saying that the German Consul at Antwerp had posted notice in his consulate inviting all exiled Jews to come back to Germany, and promising them the complete restoration of their property.

A dispatch from Los Angeles saying that the German liner Bremen, of 51,731 tons, was "hiding" in the little port of Progreso, Mexico.

A dispatch from Budapest saying that the Polish radio had announced the defeat and rout of the German army in front of Warsaw.

It will be noted that all these palpable imbecilities had one thing in common: they bore date-lines of places safely remote from the fray. There will be more and worse as the war develops, and the liars hanging about its outskirts perfect their virtuosity. Such liars were so active during all the conflicts of the recent past that some of the towns they operated in retain a sorry notoriety to this day. For example, Mole St. Nicholas, Haiti, which supplied the Ameri-

194

can papers with a daily grist of preposterous rumors throughout the war with Spain. Again, Copenhagen, which turned out a marvelous and never-failing crop of lies from August 2, 1914, to November 11, 1918. Yet again, Riga in Latvia, which specialized in prodigies and wonders from across the Russian border in the days of the Bolshevist revolution and the ensuing civil wars.

I was myself in Copenhagen late in 1916, and saw the rumor-machine there in operation, or at all events, one unit of it. This unit took the form of a somewhat frowsy Danish journalist in a padded smoking-jacket and carpet slippers. An American colleague and I, for some reason that I forget, called on him at his house, and found him hard at work. He told us that he represented both the *Berliner Tageblatt* and the London *Daily Mail.* "I give each of them," he explained, "just what it wants. I am kept jumping." He unquestionably was, and so were the American managing editors who had to deal, soon or late, with his fancies.

I am surely no apologist for the newspapers, which I have been denouncing for stupidity and worse for thirty years, but it seems to me that they are hardly to be blamed for occasionally printing such balderdash. After all, it is not easy to distinguish, in wartime, between astounding facts and simple lies. The most incredible things actually happen. The judicious may be able to distinguish, in the light of calm reflection, the fact from the lie, but a managing editor sitting at his red-hot desk has no time for calm reflection. He must decide at once, and if he sometimes falls for a whopper then let us not forget that he also detects many another, and heaves it into his wastebasket.

Every managing editor has stored away, in the concrete-mixer that passes for a heart, memories of occasions when he succumbed to the natural suspiciousness of his craft—and missed a thumping story. And even if he has contrived by Freudian means to obliterate such uncomfortable personal recollections, he recalls only too well that a colleague on an eminent New York paper, on the night of the Titanic disaster, refused to believe or print the first report of it. Also, he ponders on the satirical mirth that arose in Fleet Street when hints began to reach there, only a few weeks ago, that Stalin and Hitler were about to kiss and make up.

In the present war, it seems to me, the general accuracy of the news printed by American newspapers has reached an extraordi-

195

narily high mark. What they have printed one day has been borne out, at least four times out of five, on the day following, and when they have gone wrong in any important matter it has been the fault of some Government press agent. This circulation of false news by official liars will probably grow worse hereafter, especially after the main fighting is transferred to the Western front. The English atrocity bureau is, as yet, hardly functioning; in a little while it will be doing better. It performed marvels in the last war to save democracy, and once it gets its gait it will perform them again.

The American reporters on the other side may be divided roughly into two grand divisions—the men in the field and the imitation statesmen who operate from the capitals of the nations at war. The former, taking one with another, are hard-working and competent fellows, and it is most unusual for one of them to send false news. It is, of course, not easy in wartime to unearth the truth, and the impediments to getting it home unpolluted are often formidable. Yet there are reporters who manage to do it—and not only on rare occasions but even more or less steadily.

In *The Evening Sun* of last Thursday there were two long dispatches that showed such a reporter at work. He was Daniel De Luce—a strange name to me, as it must have been to nearly all his readers. It appeared that he was an Associated Press staff correspondent, and that he had set out from Budapest to find out what was going on in southeastern Poland, a forlorn and almost forgotten back-water of the war. His difficulties in getting to Lwow must have been tremendous, and they were even worse on his return, which took him to the Rumanian border. Yet, with his life in danger every moment, he faced and surmounted them, and on his arrival at the border he sent out by way of Bucharest the best story of the war that has been printed so far.

It had every merit, and no defects. It was vivid, it was comprehensive, and it was dispassionate. The sufferings of the fugitive Poles touched him, and he made the fact plain, but he did not linger too much over his own reactions and reflections. Instead, he applied himself undividedly to the business before him, which was to find out what was actually going on in southeastern Poland. Having made his report in the fewest possible words, without evading any natural questions or neglecting anything significant, he shut up.

196

This Mr. De Luce must be set down as extraordinary, but he is certainly not singular. On the contrary, he has many runners-up. The least of them is worth all the Government press-agents now in operation in Europe. And he is also worth all the gaudy journalistic wizards who sit in the safe hotels of unbombed capitals, and tell us, not what has happened, but what they think.

Nine times out of ten what they think is worth precisely nothing. Go back a few weeks, and recall what they were thinking then. They were all busy writing powerful essays on the forces at play behind the developing situation, and nine-tenths of those essays were hooey. Nearly every time they attempted prophecy it turned out that they were wrong, and whenever they happened to be right it was for wrong reasons. Most of them revealed bias in every line they wrote. They forgot altogether the prime duty of a journalist, which is to ascertain and tell the truth, and devoted themselves idiotically to the role of the statesman, whose job it is to make the worse reason appear the better one.

The radio companies, I am informed, have decided to clear out all the similar quacks on their own staffs, and to confine their news of the war to actual news. It would be a good idea for the newspapers and press associations to follow suit. In such times as these it is of paramount importance that the news should be as little sophisticated by prejudice and imagination as possible. There is enough official propaganda on the wires already, without the newspapers themselves hiring more and worse propagandists.

To be sure, commentaries have their value—but not commentaries by vapid and irresponsible nonentities. I suspect that the custom of signing foreign news dispatches, even press association dispatches, is responsible for the baleful proliferation of this nuisance. Perhaps it might be got rid of by setting up a simple test for war "experts" and other such grandiose "authorities." Let the right to sign the more metaphysical dispatches be restricted to men who have actually seen the war, and given proof under field conditions that they can tell a hawk from a handsaw. In other words, let it be confined to competent newspapermen.

197

31

Speech to the National Conference of Editorial Writers

(Washington, D.C., October 14, 1947)

Gentlemen, I should really apologize. I came over here under a misapprehension. I didn't know you were having a solemn meeting. I thought it was a sort of round-table and that everybody would horn in.

I have prepared nothing and have been sitting here trying to pick up some ideas. I think I should say at once that the harvest has not been very rich.

If an old editorial writer who long ago reformed may be permitted to advise his present superiors, I should say that the thing you want to discuss in this organization is the fundamental thing—that is: why have editorials at all?

Why do you give over three or four columns a day to solemn discourses—and when they are supposed to be lively they are even more solemn, in my opinion—filling three or four columns of space with the opinions of unknown and in many cases not-worth-knowing men?

An editorial, to have any rationale at all, should say something. It should take a line.

Or if you haven't any opinion, and if you don't want to take a line, don't print the editorial. You don't have to print it.

Look at these papers on this wall. They all look alike. There are two or three columns of editorials, a bad cartoon—and I say bad because there are 250 editorial cartoonists in America and not ten of them are good, and that ten are not good every day.

So you have that, and then you have a miscellany of features, chiefly fourth-rate syndicate features, terrible stuff that no sensible man would read if he could avoid it—and most can avoid it.

Now, who writes this stuff? What are you doing to train editorial writers? You are getting the wrong men, and you are handling them wrong.

An editorial writer has only one excuse for existence: that he has a positive opinion about a subject on which he is well informed, on which he knows more than the average man.

And yet all he has to say is what you could hear in any barber shop—not from the customers but from the barbers!

If your editorial writer, in writing his editorials, "takes the fence," thinking of the dangers of antagonizing somebody or other, including the publisher's wife, he can't write anything worth reading and it is not worth while hiring him. It would be better to put him to some useful labor.

But suppose he is a good man. In very many cases he is. I have known many editorial writers who met all of the specifications that one of these gentlemen was laying down for them—all except one: they didn't know anything!

We are recruiting editorial writers in a wrong way. We are recruiting them from reporters who have trouble with their legs. We are recruiting them from old-time desk men who couldn't be trusted any more to spell words right.

And we are recruiting them from the outside. What kind of men are we getting from the outside? We are getting, in the main, the literary men.

Literary men don't make good editorial writers. I have been a literary man myself for many years, and I will testify to that very gladly.

A literary man is concerned with manner. What he says is of very little importance; it is how he says it. An editorial writer is concerned with what he has to say, and with what information he has.

I am stopping in one minute, but I want to drop one idea for your future consideration: No editorial writer ought to be permitted to sit in an editorial room for month after month and year after year, contemplating his umbilicus. He ought to go out and meet people.

I have had the curious experience many times of taking editorial writers out on news stories. Why, they didn't do as well as an office boy. They didn't know the people.

I am speaking now of big city people. I realize that in small cities an editorial writer is a member of the community, and gets around, and knows people. But on the big city papers an editorial writer very frequently doesn't know anybody. He has no special information, and he doesn't know how to get it. He is merely a literary man, filling so many columns a day with what the Australians so beautifully call "bullsh."

I suggest that you gentlemen who are responsible for the state of the art in this country devote your future sessions to trying to figure out why you should print three or four columns of editorials a day. And if you can't find any reason, stop printing them. There are other things that could be printed, things that could be written by these very men that you have.

You have good men, as I said before, working at writing editorials. But it is a psychological fact that must be obvious—even to an editor—that a good man doesn't like to write anonymously, and presumably at the dictation of a publisher. Most publishers are far too dumb to have any ideas on editorial page problems. But nevertheless, whether they are really too dumb or merely negligent, most newspapermen look on them with loathing and contempt—and I believe justly so. I have known a few exceptions, but I must say it would be hard for me to name them. And, having been everything that you can be on a newspaper excepting financial editor and sporting editor, I speak with some rather wider background than most men have.

I say the thing to do is to put your editorial writers to learning something first. Let them master a subject. Let them investigate it. Let them go out and act as a reporter; but let them—instead of writing for the first page, where their expression of opinion is limited—write for the editorial page, where they can express opinions. Give them the utmost freedom, but insist that they find out something before they do it.

And then—let them sign it! I don't care if you sign "John Smith"

200

to an article; it seems more important to most people than if it is anonymous. And also, it seems a great deal more important to John Smith, and he is going to be careful with it.

I read editorials every day which, as an old hand, convinced me of one thing: the man writing them didn't like his job, was hurrying to get home or to get out, and banged them off at the quickest pace possible. He had no ideas, and he didn't express any. He merely stated what were the prevailing ideas, juggled on the point of his nose for a minute, and went home. That is not editorial writing that is worth printing.

We are spending an enormous amount of money on editorial pages in the United States, and we are getting practically nothing from most of them. Look at them on the wall here. Look at those long columns of dead editorials. Go and read them.

One of the speakers was telling you of his efforts to read them. He said he couldn't do it. I don't blame him. Neither can the reader.

Another speaker proposed that you bring the weather report and the radio program onto the editorial page, to lure the moron into reading editorials. You are wasting time on the moron. He is never going to read editorials, no matter how good they are. In fact, the better they are the less he is going to read them.

The editorial page has one aim. That is to appeal to the more intelligent reader in his more intelligent mood. In order to do that, you have got to prepare your people with the thing I have spoken of: sound information at first hand—not read in the *New Republic,* but seen.

If I had my way, no editorial writer would be allowed to stay in the office more than one continuous week. I would send him out, if only to cover a police court, so that he would get some contact with the human race. I would send him out whenever there was a big story running in the country and we had to have an opinion about it. I would let him come in with an opinion. His opinion might not be agreed to by everyone with authority, but on the whole it would.

You haven't spoken about it here, but I have often heard talk about the singularly primitive mind of the newspaper publisher. That is true. They are people of a backward mentality.

But you are forgetting something: that what so-called information and opinion is in the head of such a primitive creature was put there by his own staff. He doesn't bring in editorial ideas. He sucks them up in the office. And he ought to get better provender. He ought to be taught better ideas. He ought to be convinced that there is such a thing in the world as the difference between truth and falsehood. That is the function of the editorial writer.

When he hasn't anything to say, he ought to do what Hofmeister of the Hanover, Pennsylvania, *Sun* does. When he hasn't anything to say, he doesn't print any editorials. Why should he? It is an excellent idea.

You will find among those smaller papers everywhere a great many ideas. And you will find also among the papers that my colleague Wagner mentioned, the London papers, a great many ideas. There are very good ideas in the London *Times*. Every day it could be imitated by American papers. We are deceived by the fact that they print ads on the first page, and we assume that they are stodgy. The London *Times* is not stodgy. There is more good writing in it than in any American paper that I can call to mind, except the old New York *Sun*.

I see some venerable men here who are probably even older than I am, although I doubt that. And those of you who are aged and decrepit, as I am, remember the days of the old New York *Sun*. It had an editorial page which made no concession to novelty, to typography! Nor did any of its pages. It was one solid mass of type. But every newspaperman in America that was worth a damn read it. And there never was an editorial in the New York *Sun* of which it could be said rationally, by any sensible individual, that he couldn't read it. They were all good.

Gentlemen, I find that I am falling into the error of all us old Poloniuses, that of preaching. You don't want to hear me preach.

But I was merely trying to throw out a few ideas to direct your own thoughts. You have to choose your poison yourselves. And the main idea is to make up your own mind as to why you print editorials at all in your own paper and, having made up your mind that there ought to be editorials, try to determine how to make those editorials most informative, useful, and sensible.

I think the way to do that is to throw the editorial writer into contact with life itself. Don't let him sit in the office and become a professor. Don't let him read other papers too much. And above all, don't let him swallow the propaganda that is all over the place.

We talk of objective reporting. There is no such thing. I have been a reporter for many years, and I can tell you that no reporter worth a hoot ever wrote a purely objective story. You get a point of view in it. If your reporter is a Guild man, and it is a political story, it is New Deal propaganda. If he is an anti-Guild man, it is probably anti-New Deal propaganda.

You can't escape it. A man that is worth reading at all has opinions. He has ideas. And you are not going to improve him by trying to choke him. Let a little opinion get into your editorial columns.

In my town of Baltimore, Henry Wallace made one of his characteristic speeches last night. I see an effort made to treat him entirely objectively. I should not do it! Either as reporter or editor, I would let it be plain what Wallace looked like, what kind of people he was associating with.

Get off the record! The greatest jackass that ever was known among newspaper publishers, as you know, was Frank Munsey. Yet even Frank Munsey had an idea. He made a rule on the New York *Sun,* in his time, that no reporter could report a speech without describing what the speaker looked like, what gestures he made, his type, and so on, his voice, and the impression he apparently made; in other words, interpreting the speaker. There is nothing more deadly than the mere text of a speech.

I am glad Munsey is dead, and I hope he is in hell! Because if he were here today, and he had his reporters reporting this meeting according to that program, I am afraid I would fare badly. Thank you, gentlemen.

32

Interview with
Donald H. Kirkley

(On June 30, 1948, Donald H. Kirkley, the television editor of the *Sun,* interviewed Mencken in the Library of Congress Recording Laboratory. The following are excerpts from that interview. Some of what Mencken said was in direct response to questions from Kirkley, and some was more or less free association.)

I

Most men that escape college have a regret that pursues them, but I must confess I am much too vain to have any such regrets. I think of what I was doing when the boys in my generation were in college listening to idiot lectures and cheering football games and doing all the foolish and silly and minuscule things college boys do. I was a young reporter on the street. . . . I believe that a young newspaper reporter in a big city at that time led a life that has never been matched on earth, for romance and interest. . . . I never was a good reporter. . . . I never got a scoop in my life. They were the things that were esteemed in those days. They never seemed to me to have any sense. Most scoops were bad stories. And they were always exaggerated and played up in an idiot manner. No, I wasn't a good reporter except in one sense—that I worked. I was willing to work. I never shirked a job. . . .

One of the things that puzzles me about the modern young newspaper man is what does he do in his leisure. He has much more leisure than they did in my time. . . . I worked all the time. He works five days a week. What does he do? [Play golf and bridge?]. . . . Well, all those things would have been considered, not only degrading but impossible—psychologically—in my time. . . . The idea of a newspaper reporter with any self-respect playing golf is to me almost inconceivable.

I hear that even printers now play golf. God almighty, that's dreadful to think of. I remember printers in my time—I knew a great many intimately. I always had to do with makeup on the papers and hence I knew the printers. And I was very fond of them and they were fine fellows—but golf playing! It would just seem as incredible to hear of a printer going to a dance. Printers spent their leisure mainly in saloons and in summer on the shores down the rivers below Baltimore. They were intelligent men—the good ones. I learned a great deal more about the newspaper business from printers than I ever learned from editors. A great deal more. But now when you hear of a printer going out and dressing himself up and playing golf. The thing is really obscene. . . .

It's dreadful to think of [reporters working 40-hour weeks]. . . . You could no more have a 40-hour week for a good newspaper reporter than you could have a 40-hour week for an archbishop. It's just not possible. A good reporter . . . simply refuses to let a story go when he's got his teeth into it. And he wants assignments. I remember when I went down to the office in the morning, certainly the thing that interested me wasn't whether I would get a lot of time off and go home early but whether I'd get some good assignments. If I got the good assignments, I didn't care how long I worked. I worked many a time all night. When the Baltimore fire happened in February, 1904, I was the young city editor. They dug me out of bed about 11 o'clock in the morning and said a big fire had started downtown. I went downtown. I never got my clothes off or slept until Wednesday morning at 4 o'clock. That's from Sunday to Wednesday. I suppose that's almost the record for continuous work. I grant you that there were moments when I drowsed at my desk, but I never stretched out to sleep until Wednesday morning. And far from looking on that as oppressive or keeping an account of overtime, I was delighted with the opportunity. I was young, I was ambitious and I liked the job.

I get the impression from the modern reporter that he doesn't really like his work. He wishes he were a druggist. Or he wishes he had a good job. . . . [Or was a dramatist?] No. The reporter with literary ambitions is one that I always respected. But most of the reporters that I encounter these days haven't even got literary ambitions. They never write anything outside the office. . . .

III

I think [newspaper ownership of television stations] is a curse to newspapers and I wish it could be separated from them. I am sorry that the Federal Communications Commission did not prohibit ownership of radio stations by a newspaper. I don't think it's a good thing in the public sense for any one agency to control rival news sources. They ought to be kept separate and in active rivalry. That's one objection to it. Secondly, human nature being what it is, as soon as a television or any kind of radio enterprise gets into a newspaper, an enormous number of men—including some of the best men—become radio crooners, not newspaper men. . . . Actors. Yeah, they get stagestruck at first, that's true. And it shows in the newspaper instantly. The way for newspapers to meet the competition of radio and television is simply to get out better newspapers. They can always keep miles ahead of these other agencies which haven't the machinery for doing what newspapers can do. Newspapers ought to print better papers. They are going downhill and any time you find a newspaper that's got a radio department you'll find a newspaper that is deteriorating.